CULTURES OF THE WORLD®

PHILIPPINES

Lily Rose R. Tope/Detch P. Nonan-Mercado

BENCHMARK BOOKS

MARSHALL CAVENDISH
NEW YORK

PICTURE CREDITS

Cover photo: © Mark Downey

AFP: 31, 80 • ANA Press Agency: 5, 40, 41, 43, 47, 53 • APA: 3, 26, 27 • Bes Stock: 28 • Bosquejo Geografico E. Historico Naturel del Archipelago Filipino: 128 • Bruce Coleman Collection: 42 • Emil V. Davocol: 100 • Embassy of the Philippines, Singapore: 25, 111, 126 • Victor Englebert: 81 • Ayesha C. Ercelawn: 87 • Alain Evrard: title, 3, 8, 14, 20, 36, 39, 49, 52, 57, 62, 64, 66, 68, 70, 71, 73, 75, 78, 85, 86, 91 bottom, 95 both, 96, 97, 98, 99 both, 102, 103, 104, 105, 107, 109, 110, 114 • B.J. Formento: 4, 15, 51 bottom, 59, 65, 88, 94, 101 bottom, 122, 129 • Dave G. Houser/Houserstock: 48 • Anthony Hughes: 17 both, 29, 108 • Lopez Memorial Foundation: 93 • National Library, Philippines: 21, 22, 23 • Susan Nerney: 63 • John Pennock: 6, 7, 10, 12, 13 bottom, 16, 18, 32, 54, 60, 90, 106, 112, 115, 117 • Photobank: 116, 118, 130, 131 • Elizabeth V. Reyes: 34, 55, 69, 72, 74, 77, 79, 121, 124, 127 top • Nico G. Sepe: 38, 61, 76, 82, 92, 101 top • Bernard Sonneville: 9, 33, 67 • George C. Tapan: 51 top, 125 • Lily Rose R. Tope: 24, 50, 113 • Topham Picturepoint: 89

ACKNOWLEDGMENTS

With thanks to Ms. Minda Cruz, Minister and Consul General,
Embassy of the Republic of the Philippines, Singapore,
for her reading of this manuscript.

PRECEDING PAGE

T'boli children dressed in the indigenous fabrics and beads of their ethnic group.
The T'boli live in Davao province on Mindanao island in the Philippines.

Marshall Cavendish Corporation
99 White Plains Road
Tarrytown, NY 10591
Website: www.marshallcavendish.com

© 1990, 2002 by Times Media Private Limited
All rights reserved. First edition 1990. Second edition 2002.

Originated and designed by
Times Books International, an imprint of
Times Media Private Limited, a member of the
Times Publishing Group

Printed in Malaysia

Library of Congress Cataloging-in-Publication Data
Tope, Lily Rose R., 1955–
   Philippines / Lily Rose R. Tope, Mercado Nordilica.—2nd ed.
       p. cm.—(Cultures of the world)
   Summary: Discusses the geography, history, government, economy, people, and culture of the Philippines, an archipelago of many islands in the Western Pacific.
   Includes bibliographical references and index.
   ISBN 0-7614-1475-4
   1. Philippines—Juvenile literature. [1. Philippines.] I. Nordilica, Marcado. II. Series.
DS655.T66 2002
959.9—dc21   2002019725

765432

CONTENTS

A Filipina, all spruced up, at a town fiesta.

Zamboanga in Mindanao has been called the "City of Flowers." Here, at a local market, a boy sells the item that has made the city famous.

INTRODUCTION

THE PHILIPPINES has a rich cultural heritage. Although Philippine culture greets visitors with a strikingly Western appearance, it soon reveals a strong Asian character. A large proportion of the Filipino ("fi-li-PEE-no") population speaks English, professes Christianity, and votes for a democratic government. Filipinos are a friendly and hospitable people, united in their diverse origins from 77 ethno-linguistic groups.

The Philippines also has a rich natural environment. This archipelago in Southeast Asia is home to more than 150 mammal species and over 12,000 plant species.

On the political and social front, the Philippines is a positive example to other nations in turmoil as a nation with the ability to hope in the midst of dire poverty and the will to choose peace in times of war.

GEOGRAPHY

THE REPUBLIC OF THE PHILIPPINES is an archipelago of around 7,100 islands splayed like a necklace in the Western Pacific, separated from mainland Asia by the South China Sea. In 1751, Father Juan J. Delgado, a Jesuit historian, named the Philippines "Pearl of the Orient." Manila's galleon trade then conveyed silk, porcelain, spices, pearls, and other goods from the East to the West.

Reaching toward Taiwan in the north and almost touching Borneo in the south, the Philippine islands occupy a land area of 115,124 square miles (298,170 square km)—slightly larger than Arizona—and have a combined coastline twice the length of that of the United States. Fewer than a third of the islands are inhabited, and the largest 11 account for 95 percent of the total land area. Mountain ranges running through the island chain contrast with the green lower slopes and coastal plains.

Left: **Pangasinan province's famous "Hundred Islands" are located off the northwestern coast of Luzon. Rich in marine life, this area has the second largest collection of coral specimens in the world.**

Opposite: **Mountain ranges in Ifugao province, northern Luzon, overlook impressive rice terraces carved out of mountain slopes.**

Roxas Boulevard along Manila Bay has one of Manila's most beautiful panoramic views. The Bay provides excellent protected anchorage.

LUZON, THE VISAYAS, AND MINDANAO

The Philippines can roughly be divided into three main islands: Luzon, the Visayas, and Mindanao. Luzon, the largest island in the Philippine archipelago, is also the most populated. It includes Metro Manila, which is home to about 10 million Filipinos, and one of the world's best harbors, Manila Bay. With its strategic marine location, Manila is the most logical seat of national government and commerce.

South of Luzon is a network of islands collectively called the Visayas. The most important Visayan islands are Leyte, Negros, Samar, Panay, and Cebu. Cebu is the region's business and industrial center. In 1565, explorer Miguel López de Legaspi established the first Spanish colony in the Philippines in Cebu. In 1571, he moved the colonial base to Manila, which would become the seat of power and business for the next four centuries.

Mindanao has a healthy economy based on trade and industry, although parts of the island still lag behind Luzon and the Visayas because of poor communication links and technological infrastructure. The wide use of mobile phones and the popularity of short messaging service (SMS), known locally as mobile phone texting, has brought Mindanao residents closer to their neighbors in Cebu and Manila, the country's largest urban centers. Through SMS Filipinos throughout Mindanao are sharing ideas and sometimes even carrying out business. Meanwhile, Internet access has yet to be established in smaller cities.

QUEEN OF VOLCANOES

Mount Mayon (*right*), the Philippines' most active volcano, rises 8,000 feet (2,438 m) into the sky over southeastern Luzon. The name *mayon* comes from the Bicol word *magayon*, meaning "beautiful." (Bicol is a region made up of six provinces: Albay, Camarines Norte, Camarines Sur, Catanduanes, Masbate, and Sorsogon.) Mayon still has a beautiful, almost perfect conical shape, even after at least 47 eruptions in the last 385 years. Despite the obvious danger, farmers cultivate rice up to 5 miles (8 km) from the volcano.

The first recorded Mayon eruption was in 1616. The most devastating eruption occurred in 1814, burying nearby towns in mudflow and ash and claiming more than 2,000 lives. Only the bell of the church tower remains as a reminder of Mayon's wrath. The volcano last unleashed its fury in February 2000, displacing some 80,000 people.

Taal Lake and volcano at dawn, seen from Tagaytay Ridge. Situated on an island in the center of Taal Lake (which itself is the crater of an extinct volcano), Taal is the lowest active volcano in the world and has been the most destructive in Philippine history.

LAND OF FIRE AND HEAVING EARTH

The geological birth of the Philippine archipelago was the result of volcanic activity and the movement of tectonic plates. These processes led to the formation of islands, mountains, and oceanic trenches in many parts of the world, but few events were this dramatic. In the case of much of the Philippine archipelago, coral, which thrives in the warm waters where the islands lie, accumulated in ancient times to form the foundations of the islands.

During the Ice Age, land bridges connected the Philippine islands to other islands in the region and to the Asian continent. These bridges provided a path for the spread of terrestrial wildlife. Today, as a result, there are similarities in flora and fauna found in the Philippines and in Sulawesi (Celebes), the Moluccas, Borneo, and even Taiwan, although these countries are now separated by large bodies of water.

While nature has blessed the Philippines with abundant natural resources, it has also cursed the country with a sometimes dangerous and unpredictable environment. The Philippines lies in a zone of earth fractures around the Pacific Ocean that is prone to earthquakes. The archipelago also forms a link in a volcanic belt known as the Pacific "Ring of Fire," which coincides with the edges of the Pacific plate, where more than half of the world's active above-sea level volcanoes lie.

The Philippines experiences one large-magnitude (7.75 or higher on the Richter Scale) tectonic earthquake every 10 years, seven earthquakes of major magnitude (7.0 to 7.4) every 10 years, and five earthquakes of moderate magnitude (6.0 to 6.9) every year. There are some 21 active volcanoes distributed throughout the Philippine archipelago; the major ones are Mayon, Taal, Hibok-Hibok, and Kanlaon.

Although volcanic eruptions have caused extensive damage in the country, they have also been responsible for the superior quality of Philippine soil. In addition, volcanoes are an excellent source of thermal energy.

The Philippine Institute of Volcanology and Seismology studies earthquakes and volcanic activity in the Philippines, gathering information to help predict earthquakes and eruptions and avert the potentially disastrous results.

In 1991, together with the U.S. Geological Survey (USGS), the institute successfully forecast the Mount Pinatubo eruption. The timely evacuation of people living near the volcano saved thousands of lives.

There are more than 200 volcanoes in the Philippines. Most are extinct or dormant, such as Mount Arayat in Pampanga province. Dormant volcanoes can wake up anytime. Mount Pinatubo, for example, erupted violently in 1991 after half a century of sleep. Volcanic eruptions in the Philippines often cause tsunami, and heavy rains that commonly lead to mudflows.

A quay destroyed by a typhoon in southwestern Luzon.

CLIMATE

The Philippines is generally warm and wet, with temperatures ranging from 75°F to 88°F (24°C to 31°C) and an average annual rainfall of 80 inches (2,030 mm). Seasons may be classified as hot, rainy, or cool. The hot and dry season lasts from March through June; July begins the wet season, with frequent rains until October; and from November to February, the weather is pleasantly cool and dry.

TYPHOONS The typhoon is a strong tropical cyclone equivalent to the hurricane in North and Central America. Typhoons are characterized by air spinning violently in a counter-clockwise direction and a calm core called the "eye." Typhoons often travel in a slightly curved path as they pass over land, but they are also known to turn back, not only once but several times, or to mysteriously tarry.

In the Philippines typhoons are given signal values to indicate their intensity. Signal One means windspeeds are less than 39 miles per hour (63 km per hour); Signal Two labels windspeeds from 39 to 54 miles per hour (63 to 87 km per hour); and Signal Three covers windspeeds above 54 miles per hour (above 87 km per hour). Elementary and intermediate grades in school are suspended during Signal Two winds, while Signal Three winds call for all classes to be suspended and people to stay indoors. Typhoons occur in the months of the southwest monsoon, often bringing heavy rains, floods, and even gigantic waves as they hit land. In a typical year, 21 typhoons strike the Philippines, affecting nearly 700,000 people, damaging more than 7,000 buildings, and destroying agricultural crops.

FLORA

The Philippines is one of the world's richest wildlife havens. More than 12,000 species of plants are found in the Philippines. Of the flowering plants, the orchid family is the largest with about 940 species, 790 native. The coastal mangrove swamps are also covered with lush plant growth. The rain forests total 57,915 square miles (150,000 square km), nearly half the country's land.

ABACA This plant from the banana family is known as Manila hemp. The stem of the abaca is stripped lengthwise and made into rope and fabric. Foreign seamen in the 19th century discovered the tensile strength of abaca fibers and its ability to withstand the corrosiveness of seawater.

COCONUT The coconut palm is called the tree of life because of its versatility. Humans have found a use for every part of the palm, from its deepest root to its farthest frond—for food and drink, for building roofs and walls, for fuel, and for making products such as jewelry, mattresses, and paper. In colloquial Filipino, the brain is referred to as the coconut, as in the expression "use your coconut."

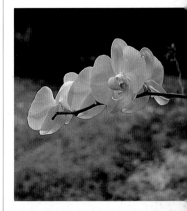

Orchids and coconuts grow profusely in the Philippines. The first coconut was believed to have been brought over from mainland Asia during the Neolithic period.

FAUNA

The monkey-eating eagle, called "air's noblest flier" by aviator Charles Lindbergh, is one of the world's rarest birds. It stands over three feet (0.9 m) tall and has a wingspan of nearly eight feet (2.4 m).

Some species of animals in the Philippines are similar to those found on other islands in the region, particularly in Borneo and Java. Ancient land bridges enabled the migration of wildlife around Southeast Asia, while traders and conquerors brought foreign species from farther afield to the Philippines. The archipelago has about 800 bird species, and its reefs are famous for their size and diverse marine life. Although a considerable number of animal species inhabit the Philippines, each is represented by a small number. One reason may be that there are so many islands forming unique ecosystems.

Unfortunately, humans are also responsible for the scarcity of many animal species in the Philippines. Many animals known to exist only in the Philippines are now recognized as endangered or threatened. The monkey-eating eagle, the largest of all eagles, is the object of worldwide concern. Declared the national bird of the Philippines in 1995, this eagle is barely surviving deforestation. Other animals in danger of extinction are a deep forest bird called Koch's Pitta, the mouse deer, the pelican, the Sarus crane, and the nocturnal tarsier, the smallest primate.

Certain animals support human activity directly and substantially. To Filipino peasants the most important animal is the carabao, or water buffalo. Capable of backbreaking work and very patient, the carabao is the symbol of Filipino industriousness and perseverance. The smaller and wilder cousin of the carabao, the tamaraw, can be found only on the island of Mindoro.

METRO MANILA

One of the biggest and most modern city networks in Asia, Metro Manila is a metropolis of 10 cities: Caloocan, Las Piñas, Makati, Malabon, Manila, Muntinlupa, Parañaque, Pasay, Quezon, and San Juan.

The old city of Manila was for centuries the nation's capital. However, in 1937 the president, Manuel Quezon, perhaps alarmed at the crowding in Manila and a rising crime rate, decided to create a new capital in spacious, suburban Quezon. Quezon was officially the capital of the Philippines from 1948 to 1976. But Manila's historical importance could not be ignored. In 1976, Manila regained its former status as the nation's capital.

Makati is the nation's business center. The most important towns in Metro Manila are Alabang, San Pedro, Novaliches, and Valenzuela—all industrial towns.

Ayala Avenue in Makati is called the Wall Street of the Philippines.

HISTORIC MANILA

The remains of a centuries-old convent in Intramuros sit beside a new building designed in the old style.

Legend has it that Manila, known in early times as *Maynilad* ("My-NEE-lahd"), was named after the *nilad* ("NEE-lahd") plant floating on the Pasig River. Blessed with a fine harbor, Manila attracted explorers, traders, and settlers. It was already a thriving community when Miguel López de Legaspi arrived in the 1560s. He built turreted walls 33 feet (10 m) thick around the city and turned it into a fortress surrounded by moats. He called the city Intramuros, "within the walls."

Except for a two-year British interlude, the walled city was the Spanish empire's political, commercial, and cultural center in the East. When the Americans arrived in 1898, the city had outgrown its walls, leaving Intramuros a mere district.

Manila is the traditional seat of political power. Colonial governors and Philippine presidents have resided in the Malacañang Palace by the Pasig River. Significant events have taken place in Manila, such as the execution in 1896 of José Rizal; the birth of the Philippine Republic in 1948; and more recently, the rise of "people power," which replaced Ferdinand Marcos with Corazon Aquino as president and later Joseph Estrada with Gloria Arroyo.

Manila has had its share of natural and historical catastrophes. In fact, during World War II, it was the world's most devastated city after Warsaw. Despite these events, Manila has survived and persisted. Like old wine, it has acquired more flavor with age.

Mactan islanders reenact the historic battle against the Spanish.

MAJOR CITIES

CEBU Known as the Queen City of the South, Cebu is the most important city in the Visayas and the regional center of commercial and intellectual activity. Cebu city is the capital of Cebu province, whose soil is not good for farming, but perfect for industrial development. On the nearby island of Mactan, Ferdinand Magellan was defeated in battle in 1521 by a local chieftain named Lapu-Lapu. A large wooden cross left by Magellan in 1521 now stands in a plaza in commemoration of the Spanish arrival.

A statue of Lapu-Lapu stands in Cebu as a symbol of independence.

DAVAO Davao is the largest city in Mindanao and the third largest in the Philippines. It is famous for its fruit: durians, mangosteens, oranges, pomelos, bananas, and lanzones, a fruit with leathery skin and juicy, sweet-sour flesh. The early Davao inhabitants were the Manobo, famous for their exotic dress and musical instruments. Davao is now home to several ethnic groups, including the Bicolano, Cebuano, Ilocano, Ilonggo, and Tagalog.

BAGUIO Called the summer capital of the Philippines, Baguio rests on a 4,900-foot (1,494-m) plateau in the Cordillera mountains. Its pine tree-lined roads and cool highland temperatures averaging 65°F (18°C) attract world-weary lowlanders.

HISTORY

THE AETA, or Negrito, was once considered the Philippine Adam. More recent theories propose that this small-built, dark-skinned, curly-haired people migrated to the islands from Southeast Asia more than 22,000 years ago by way of land bridges.

Artifacts discovered in areas populated by Aeta communities in the Philippines indicate that the Aeta initially lived in the lowlands. One theory proposes the later arrival of peoples of Malay origin, who pushed the Aeta into the hills and mountains. The newer immigrants established communities along the sea and rivers. Before long, they developed a lifestyle all their own.

Early records indicate the existence of an advanced civilization sustained by rice culture, fishing, mining, weaving, and trading before the Spanish arrival in the Philippines.

Pre-Spanish Filipinos organized themselves in kinship-based communities called *barangay* ("ba-RUNG-gai")*, the name of the seaworthy vessel on which they traveled to the islands. They followed laws, were governed by a council of elders, and worshiped their ancestors as well as the natural forces around them. They used a form of Indic writing inscribed on bamboo and a shell currency to trade.

The influence of foreign traders enriched indigenous lifestyles. From the Chinese, the early Filipinos acquired the use of porcelain and culinary tools and learned new methods of agriculture. The Indians enriched their language and script. The Arabs brought Islam, which took root in southern Mindanao.

Despite their cosmopolitan exposure, however, the pre-Spanish Filipinos had petty kinship rivalries that divided them. The Spaniards could not have chosen an easier people to colonize.

Above: **Early inhabitants migrated across land bridges once linking the Philippines to Southeast Asia.**

Opposite: **The ruins of Dingras Church, built in 1598 in Ilocos Norte.**

Magellan's Cross at Plaza Santa Cruz, Cebu, commemorates a cross built by Ferdinand Magellan when King Humabon and Queen Juana of Cebu, together with some 800 of their subjects, were baptized.

THE SPANISH CROSS AND SWORD FOR GOD AND GOLD

In search of another route to the Spice Islands, Ferdinand Magellan sailed for the unknown Indies and landed in the Philippines on March 16, 1521. Accompanied by priests, he set up a colony and converted the local chieftains and their families to Christianity.

Five years later, the Spaniards launched a more determined expedition, headed by Miguel López de Legaspi. Equipped with his experience as a conquistador and official in Mexico, Legaspi succeeded in establishing a strong foothold in Luzon and the Visayas. He named the islands the Philippines in honor of King Philip II of Spain. Legaspi defeated the petty chieftains and rewarded those who participated in the Spanish conquests with vast tracts of land, huge estates that would later be the workplace of indigenous farmers and provide the Spaniards with comfortable living and prominent social status.

Spain ruled the Philippines via Mexico. Huge bulky ships called galleons plied between Manila and Acapulco loaded with silk, porcelain, gold, and spices bound for Europe, bringing unmeasured prosperity to investors.

The Spaniards' position in the islands was strengthened by the priests who, convinced they had to save the islands' pagan souls, embarked on a rigorous and sometimes brutal conversion campaign, baptizing the majority of the lowlanders within a short time. Social activities in the towns centered on churches built by the friars, who equaled and often surpassed the civil government in influence and power. Church and State remained entangled in the Philippines for three centuries. The Spaniards were hard taskmasters. They imposed forced labor on the indigenous people, derogatorily calling them Indios, and demanded unreasonable tributes from them. Even the clergy were known to be abusive.

Meek as they were, the Indios were often pushed to revolt but were easily quelled by the Spaniards' superior arms and "divide-and-rule" tactics. It was not until the 1800s that some form of sustained movement for social and political freedom was started. With the rise of a middle class, the sons of rich families acquired a European education and, consequently, liberal ideas. They worked to bring about reforms and held strong anti-clerical views. Among them, José Rizal stood out, with his non-violent, reformist approach. His arrest and execution in 1896 fueled the fires of a revolution led by Andres Bonifacio, the founder of a secret anti-Spanish organization called Katipunan, or Brotherhood. Killed in the revolt, Bonifacio was replaced by Emilio Aguinaldo, and on June 12, 1898, the first Philippine Republic was proclaimed.

Andres Bonifacio (1863 –97), an ardent nationalist with a humble background, advocated armed revolution.

JOSÉ RIZAL

Born June 19, 1861, in Calamba, Laguna, José Rizal (*right*) was a man of extraordinary talent and genius. A medical doctor by training, he was also a poet, musician, architect, scientist, businessman, and more. He spoke several languages, including English, Spanish, Tagalog, and Chinese. His mother, Teodora Alonso, was a great influence in his life. Her imprisonment by the Spanish authorities based on a false accusation kindled in Rizal's young heart anger against all forms of injustice. He advocated reforms in the Spanish government, though he never called for Philippine independence.

Rizal wrote two novels that exposed the abuses of the Spanish government and clergy: *Noli me Tangere* (*Touch Me Not*), published in English as *The Lost Eden*, and *El Filibusterismo* (*The Reign of Greed*), published in English as *The Subversives*. On December 30, 1896, he was arrested and publicly executed by a firing squad in Manila (*top*), after being found guilty of inciting a Katipunan insurrection that he had had no connection with. His name became the battlecry in the fight for independence.

THE AMERICAN ADVENTURE

The republic was short-lived, and rebel leader Aguinaldo was exiled. In the meantime, the Spanish-American war broke out. In 1898 U.S. Commodore George Dewey sailed into Manila Bay and destroyed the depleted Spanish naval fleet.

The Philippines sided with the United States, in hopes of gaining independence. But after losing the war, Spain ceded the Philippines to the United States for $20 million. Aguinaldo then proclaimed a republic, which the United States refused to acknowledge. So in 1899 the Philippines went to war with the United States.

Aguinaldo was captured in 1901 and the Philippine-American war finally ended in 1902, the lure of education-for-all and economic opportunities too strong to resist. The United States viewed its term in the Philippines as preparation for the country's independence. The Americans introduced U.S. political institutions and processes and opened the

A group portrait of General Aguinaldo and his fellow Filipino patriots in exile in Hong Kong in 1898.

Philippine market to the West to build economic self-sufficiency. Most important, classrooms were built to educate Filipinos. Where the Spaniards refused to educate the local people "for their own good," the Americans made education compulsory.

By 1934 the promise of a Commonwealth by 1936 and independence by 1946 had been made to Manuel Quezon, who would later become the first president of the Commonwealth. The transition would have been smooth had the Japanese not intervened.

THE THOMASITES

In 1901 a converted cattle ship called *Thomas* arrived in the Philippines from the United States, carrying 540 teachers. A smaller group had landed two months earlier to supplement soldiers who had stayed as teachers after their tours of duty. However, the Thomasites were the largest single group of teachers sent to educate and civilize their "little brown brothers." In their first 20 months in the islands, 27 Thomasites died of tropical diseases or were killed by bandits. Yet many stayed permanently and gave their time and talent to the cause of nation-building. The American system of universal education gave Filipino children (*above*) access to knowledge and spread the English language throughout the Philippines.

JAPANESE INVASION AND THE AFTERMATH

On December 10, 1941, three days after the bombing of Pearl Harbor, Japanese forces landed in the Philippines. The 12,000 Philippine Scouts and 16,000 U.S. soldiers under General Douglas MacArthur, deprived of reinforcements from the United States following the destruction of Pearl Harbor, could not stop the relentless advance of the Japanese into Manila. MacArthur's forces put up a last line of defense at Bataan and Corregidor. Forced to retreat in 1942, MacArthur pledged, "I shall return," a promise that Filipinos never forgot. He made good on this promise in 1944 when, aided by Filipino resistance fighters, U.S. forces reached the capital and defeated the Japanese in their fiercest battle, which claimed 60,000 lives and almost leveled Manila to the ground. Immediately after the war, on July 4, 1946, the Philippines was granted independence with Manuel Roxas at the helm. Extensive rehabilitation was the top priority, but with an empty treasury, the Philippines had to seek financial help from the

United States. Thus began the love-hate economic relationship between the Philippines and the United States, a factor that was to shape Philippine policy in the years to come. There were also rumblings of dissent from peasants clamoring for agrarian justice. Defense Secretary—and later president—Ramón Magsaysay distinguished himself by quelling the unrest. His ability to identify with the people and his concern for their problems restored public confidence in the government.

Rusting cannons at Corregidor are some of the relics of war on this island fortress guarding the entrance to Manila Bay. They are mute testament to the memories of Filipino and American forces who gave their lives defending the fortress.

POWER TO THE PEOPLE

Corazon Aquino's presidency (1986–92) reinstated democracy and improved the economy.

In 1965 Ferdinand Marcos was elected president. In 1969 he became the first president to be reelected. An astute statesman, Marcos rallied the people with his vow to make the Filipino great again. But his early achievements were soon eroded by the excesses of his latter years in office.

On September 21, 1972, amid nationwide dissent, Marcos declared martial law. He jailed or exiled his opponents, installed media controls, abolished the congress, force-ratified the 1973 constitution, and established his New Society Movement. Marcos and his wife, Imelda, isolated themselves and depleted the nation's coffers with their extravagant lifestyle.

On August 21, 1983, Benigno Aquino, Marcos' exiled political rival, returned to the Philippines and was assassinated on the airport tarmac. His death sparked widespread protest. In January 1986, Aquino's widow, Corazon, challenged Marcos in a snap election. Minister of Defense Juan Ponce Enrile and Vice Chief of Staff Fidel Ramos defected to Aquino's side on February 22. Millions of people trekked to the military camps to protect the defectors from Marcos' forces. Three days later, Marcos left for a Hawaiian exile. The "people power" revolution demonstrated that change could be achieved through peaceful means.

In 2001, "people power" removed Joseph Estrada from the presidency. Estrada entered politics in 1969, at the height of his movie career. He was mayor of San Juan, a Manila suburb, for 16 years. In 1987, he became senator, then vice-president in 1992, and president in 1998. Barely three years later, he faced impeachment charges, including bribery, betrayal of public trust, and violation of the constitution. In January 2001, Estrada stepped down after a string of generals and cabinet members abandoned his administration.

Vice-president Gloria Arroyo, a U.S.-trained economist, assumed the presidency in a peaceful revolution that earned the Philippines a Nobel Peace Prize. Arroyo was Undersecretary of Trade and Industry during Aquino's term. She was elected senator in 1992 and was reelected in 1995. In 1998, she was elected vice-president.

Arroyo's approach to running the country is based on fighting poverty and improving moral standards in government and society.

A TIME OF TERROR

In addition to persistent economic problems, Arroyo has had to grapple with terrorism. Her government has taken military action against the Abu Sayyaf, a hostile rebel group fighting for an independent Muslim state in the south. The Abu Sayyaf gained international recognition in 2000 when it held 21 people hostage on Jolo island until the Estrada government paid them a ransom. The Abu Sayyaf has ties with Osama bin Laden's Al-Qaeda network responsible for the bombing of the World Trade Center in the United States. The Arroyo government has refused negotiations with the Abu Sayyaf, vowing to crush the group.

Gloria Arroyo, the 14th president of the Philippines.

27

GOVERNMENT

PHILIPPINE DEMOCRACY suffered a setback during the Marcos years. In 1987, during the presidency of Corazon Aquino, the constitution was revised to mandate a presidential system of government with three independent branches: the executive, which administers the government; the legislative, which enacts laws; and the judicial, which enforces justice.

Executive power is vested in the president, who is head of state and commander-in-chief of the armed forces. Assisted by a cabinet, the president serves one six-year term and can approve or veto bills passed by the legislative branch, the congress. The congress has two chambers: the Senate (24 members popularly elected to serve six-year terms) and the House of Representatives (250 members serving three-year terms). The judiciary consists of the Supreme Court (one chief justice and 14 associate justices appointed by the president) and its lower courts, and the court of appeals (one presiding justice and 68 associate justices).

Left: **The neoclassical Congress Building in Manila houses the Senate.**

Opposite: **Baguio military academy cadets parade on Independence Day.**

LOCAL ADMINISTRATION

The national government is centered in the capital, Manila, but greater autonomy is being given to local governments. At least two regions, the Cordillera and southern Mindanao, have been given full autonomy. City governments are autonomous and are run by mayors. There are more than 60 cities.

The highest local unit is the province, which is run by a governor. Each province consists of several districts, each of which has a representative in the congress. Each district, in turn, is divided into municipalities. There are more than 1,500 municipalities in the country. Headed by a mayor, the municipality consists of territories called *barangay*. There are more than 40,000 *barangay* in the country, each governed by a chairperson.

GRASSROOTS GOVERNANCE

The *barangay* of old traveled the waters of the archipelago, each holding 60 to 90 people.

The word *barangay* describes the sea vessels used by the early settlers. Originally, it also connoted a kinship group. Each *barangay* was headed by a *datu* ("DHAH-to"), the most prominent man in the village. He was assisted by a council of elders who saw to it that the people in the community observed the ancient laws.

During Spanish rule, the *barangay* chiefs became the representatives of the civil government on a local level. Today, the modern *barangay*, or township, is the basic political unit. The *barangay* government has executive, legislative, and adjudicatory powers defined by the Local Government Code.

A chairperson and seven council members lead the *barangay*. These are elected by the township to a three-

year term, and they cannot serve more than three consecutive terms in the same office. They meet with officials of other *barangay* in their municipality in the association of *barangay* councils.

The *barangay* council plans and implements policies at the township level. It also plans development programs according to the needs of the township, mobilizes participation in national and local programs, and evaluates the implementation of these programs. The *barangay* supports the youth of the township with scholarships for the poor and by encouraging civic association membership, where the youth receive instruction in useful trades to help them earn a living.

Provincial leaders meet the National Security Adviser Secretary (*third from left*) at the Mindanao Dialogue for Understanding and Peace.

ECONOMY

A TRAINED ECONOMIST, Gloria Arroyo offered her people the first glimmer of hope for their poverty-stricken country when she assumed the presidency. By the time Arroyo took office, the Philippine economy had been seriously neglected for some time, the result of national unrest during the latter part of Estrada's term.

Following the attempted impeachment of the former president, foreign investors began pulling out of the country. Economic growth fell to 3.1 percent in the first nine months of 2001, down from 4.1 percent in the same period in 2000. Arroyo needs all her experience in money matters as she struggles to put the Philippines on the path to economic recovery and to win back investor confidence.

A slowdown in the U.S. economy made her task even harder, since about 30 percent of Philippine exports go to the United States.

Left: **The port of Manila handles both domestic and international trade.**

Opposite: **The Philippines is chiefly an agricultural country. Much farmland is devoted to rice, corn, sugarcane, and coconut plantations.**

Most commercial fishing takes place off the islands of Palawan, Mindanao, Negros, and Panay.

ECONOMIC SECTORS

Agriculture in the Philippines is a major economic sector, contributing 20 percent of the gross domestic product (GDP) and employing 40 percent of the labor force. The country's soil, enriched by volcanic ash, supports a wide range of crops, such as rice, corn, sugarcane, bananas, and pineapples. Coastal and inland waters, with more than 2,400 species of fish, make good fishing grounds. Cattle and poultry farms produce beef, pork, and eggs. In 2001 the agricultural sector grew by 4 percent.

The industrial sector includes food processing, electronics assembly, and the production of textiles and pharmaceuticals. In the first six months of 2001, this sector grew by 2.7 percent, a steep decline from a rate of 3.9 percent in the same period the previous year.

Public and private services contribute nearly half the GDP and employ 37 percent of the labor force. In January 2002 the social service subsector was given the biggest share (30 percent) of the national budget.

INTERNATIONAL TRADE

Besides the United States, the Philippines' other main trading partners are Japan, the Netherlands, Singapore, the United Kingdom, and Hong Kong. Canada and Australia are smaller trading partners.

Trade with the United States includes exports of sugar, electronic components, and apparel and clothing accessories; and imports of consumer goods and food products such as poultry, fruit and vegetables, breakfast cereals, and chocolates.

To make the export sector more competitive, the Department of Trade and Industry, together with private corporations and other government departments, aims to group related industries into "clusters" as part of the Philippine Export Development Plan for 2002 through 2004.

The Philippines joined the World Trade Organization (WTO) in 1995 and is also a member of the Asia-Pacific Economic Cooperation (APEC) and the Association of Southeast Asian Nations (ASEAN).

DRUG TRAFFICKING

In 2001, there were some 1.8 million illegal drug users in the Philippines. The Philippines is a producer of cannabis for the global trade in illicit drugs. But the most popular drug is methamphetamine hydrochloride, known as shabu, smuggled in from southern China by boat.

President Arroyo has ordered a campaign to uncover the country's intricate drug trafficking network. Government officials have been linked to this network. (In October 2001, the mayor of a Quezon town was caught in a municipality ambulance carrying some 1,100 pounds (about 500 kg) of shabu, valued at about US$20 million.) The Philippine and Chinese governments have agreed to share information on drug cases and criminals in the war against the transnational drug trade.

The stability of the region will not depend on the military presence of superpowers. It is economic cooperation and a common vision of what the region should be ... as well as what the condition of the world could be in terms of the reduction of weapons of mass destruction.

—Fidel V. Ramos

THE JEEPNEY, DESCENDANT OF THE JEEP

Visitors who ride in a jeepney (*above*) get a fleeting feel of the Filipino lifestyle. King of Philippine roads, the jeepney is an elongated, more colorful, and localized version of the American World War II jeep. Each jeepney can carry 16 passengers comfortably, although it may ferry more in areas where transportation is limited. There are three entrances: two front doors for the driver and two passengers and one at the back leading to the main passenger area. Flamboyant colors, decorations such as flags and curtains, and blaring stereo music make the jeepney a mini fiesta on wheels. The sides of the jeepney are painted with colorful images of rockets, the planets, or whatever the driver likes. There may be a tiny altar hanging at the top of the windshield or on the rearview mirror. The driver etches the names of his family on the dashboard. A board covered with posters of movie stars separates the driver from the passenger compartment, where standing passengers can keep themselves from falling off the jeepney by holding on to two parallel bars running close to the ceiling.

Burnham Park in Baguio is a tranquil getaway for tourists and locals.

TOURISM

The Philippines' tourism offices around the world promote the country as a tourist destination. Word-of-mouth recommendations by satisfied visitors also help attract tourists, while Filipinos working abroad encourage their friends to visit.

Recognition of significant attractions by world organizations such as the United Nations Educational, Scientific and Cultural Organization (UNESCO) alerts travelers to must-see sites. For example, in 1992 the UNESCO World Heritage List included four Philippine churches as fine examples of baroque art. The Puerto-Princesa Subterranean River National Park, with the longest underground river in the world, was added to the list in 1999.

The rice terraces around Banaue, the Chocolate Hills of Bohol, the port city of Cebu, and thousands of uninhabited islands are other places for tourists to explore. The challenge in promoting tourism to nature sites is to protect the environment from possible damage caused by tourism.

Filipinos are a highly literate people, and English is the business lingua franca.

THE LABOR FORCE

The Philippines has a literacy rate of 94.6 percent. Yet, unable to sustain steady economic growth, the country cannot generate enough jobs to employ a labor force of 48.1 million, including the thousands who graduate from universities every year.

Many Filipinos leave home, braving the uncertainties of life in a foreign country, to secure a more stable source of income abroad to support themselves and their families. Filipinos work as doctors, nurses, and engineers in the Middle East and as domestic helpers in Hong Kong, Singapore, and some European cities. Filipino entertainers spice up the nightlife in Japan.

The Philippines has a large pool of skilled labor, and a relative proficiency in English makes Filipinos internationally marketable. Employment prospects in developed countries are bright for skilled workers, professionals, and especially information technology specialists as the knowledge-based economy continues to expand.

CORPORATE CULTURE

Filipinos are cordial at work. While Westerners may prefer to get straight to the point in a business meeting, Filipinos generally enjoy small talk and refreshments before getting down to business. Establishing personal relationships and the right atmosphere for negotiation is a necessary part of doing business in the Philippines. Because of this, deals tend to be made more slowly in the Philippines than in the United States. Also, Filipinos seek group consensus for decisions.

Filipinos place a lot of value on their self-esteem, or *amor propio* ("ah-MOR PRO-pio"), and get upset when criticized in front of other people. The way to deal with Filipino co-workers is to point out their mistakes in private and close cheerfully by enquiring about the family. In general, to avoid embarassment, Filipinos do not openly disagree with or turn down another person. They may say "yes" when they really mean "I'll think about it" or even "no." The only way to be sure about an agreement is to get it in writing.

Some offices in the Philippines resemble large, extended households or urban villages, with the boss as the head of the family or the chief. Everyone knows everyone else, and coffee breaks are a time to catch up on the latest office romance or to plan an outing after work. Filipinos also chat on the job, a way of acknowledging the presence of their colleagues, no matter how urgent the task at hand. Teasing superiors is a way of personalizing professional relationships and establishing camaraderie.

Smooth interpersonal relationships are the Filipino way of life, at home and at work.

39

ENVIRONMENT

THE PHILIPPINES RANKS EIGHTH among the world's countries in biological diversity. There are more than 10,000 species of flowering plants and ferns in the Philippines, at least 739 species of birds, and more than 2,000 varieties of fish.

It is estimated that less than 20 percent of the Philippines is forested today, compared to a forest cover of nearly 60 percent in the early 1930s.

Despite efforts by the government to conserve the nation's forests, the Philippines has one of the highest rates of deforestation in the world—some 7 square miles (19 square km) a day. Forestry experts predict that at this rate, the country may be left with less than 7 percent of virgin forests by 2010 and none at all by 2025.

Other environmental threats come from factory and vehicle emissions that pollute water and air and fishing practices that destroy coral reefs.

The urgency of environmental conservation in the Philippines is underscored by economic incentives for maintaining the country's biodiversity—a rich, unique natural environment has the potential to earn the nation foreign exchange through ecotourism. It also offers a live laboratory for scientific research, which may lead to discoveries of new species of plants and animals.

The Philippine Department of Environment and Natural Resources (DENR) is the main government body responsible for the conservation, management, and development of the country's natural environment.

Above: **The binturong has been declared a vulnerable species in the Philippines.**

Opposite: **Clear waters off Palawan province.**

IN DANGER OF EXTINCTION

Among rare or critically endangered endemic species in the Philippines are the Mindoro dwarf buffalo, Visayan warty pig, Walden's hornbill, Hazel's forest frog, golden-crowned flying fox, and Philippine pond turtle.

The dugong (*below*), or sea cow, and the Philippine eagle are considered vulnerable species. The dugong, once common throughout the Philippine archipelago, is now believed to inhabit mainly the waters off Palawan. Threats to the survival of the dugong include accidental capture in fishing nets and hunting. Dugong meat used to be sold openly. Although its sale has now been outlawed, there are still illegal vendors of dugong meat. The World Wildlife Fund in the Philippines runs a dugong adoption program to encourage members of the public to pledge financial support for the conservation of this species.

There are fewer than 200 Philippine eagles. Called *haring ibon* ("HAH-reeng ee-BON") in Tagalog, this eagle stands up to 3.3 feet (1 m) in height and has a wingspan of almost 7 feet (2 m). It feeds on small animals such as lemurs and has an imposing arched bill and a crest of pointed crown feathers. A pair of Philippine eagles can occupy a territory of 23 to 39 square miles (60 to 100 square km).

GREENING THE ENVIRONMENT

In line with the government's strategy of sustainable development and with the cooperation of many other government agencies, the DENR has implemented forest renewal and rehabilitation projects. Reforestation forms a major part of such projects. The inhabitants in deforested areas plant fast-growing trees—to obtain useful materials such as fuel—and more permanent trees—to protect the land from erosion and flooding. Such programs aim not so much to recreate forests as to help poor communities make a living while rehabilitating the forest.

The Philippines has received external support in the form of environmental loans from organizations such as the Asian Development Bank and foreign countries such as Japan to reforest lands denuded by logging and slash-and-burn agriculture.

The Chocolate Hills. The Philippines faces an urgent need to protect its forests if Filipinos are to continue enjoying green views in the future.

43

A resort on Pangulasian Island in northern Palawan. Holiday makers are attracted to the white sands and coral reefs that make Pangulasian a good place for sunbathing and snorkeling. But these natural treasures may be lost forever without sustained coastal conservation efforts.

GUARDING THE COASTS

The 11,433-mile (18,400-km) Philippine coastline is the feeding and breeding grounds for fish and marine mammals and reptiles. Reefs bordering the coastline serve as a habitat for some 488 species of coral, 2,000 species of fish, and more than 10,000 invertebrate species. Some marine protected areas (MPAs) in the Philippines are the Tubbataha National Marine Park and Mabini Municipal Marine Reserve in Batangas. These MPAs form part of a global network of protected marine areas that includes Australia's Great Barrier Reef.

The Sulu Fund, a group of marine conservationists working to create marine parks and implement research and public education projects, conducts workshops with local fishermen in the Tubbataha National Marine Park, home of the largest reef in the Philippines.

The Philippines is also collaborating with Malaysia to run the Turtle Islands Heritage Protected Area (TIHPA). This conservation area aims to ensure the survival of sea turtles that nest in nine islands between the two countries. The coral reefs surrounding these islands also host a variety of fish and invertebrate species.

Philippine waters also support mangroves, mostly in Mindanao. The country's mangrove forests produce 108,000 tons (108 million kg) of fish annually, and many mangrove areas have been converted to fish ponds for aquaculture. Government-funded, foreign-aided projects have been implemented over the years to monitor the conditions of the country's mangrove habitats. The government involves local communities in protecting and rehabilitating denuded mangrove areas. Residents are allowed to fish and to harvest wood, but they are also taught about the economic and ecological value of mangroves.

For its efforts in attaining sustainable use of natural resources in its surroundings, the community gains stewardship over the mangrove. The government grants a mangrove stewardship certificate for a 25-year-period, renewable for another 25 years, during which the community is to take care of the coastal forest and replant mangroves.

MINDING THE MINES

Mineral wealth is another source of Philippine pride. The country has metallic reserves of gold, copper, nickel, silver, and cobalt and non-metallic reserves of limestone and marble. While the mining industry has consistently been a significant source of revenue, it has also been a major threat to the environment. The Philippine Mining Act of 1995 was enacted to tackle the problems of extensive vegetation clearing and soil erosion, mine waste, and toxic tailings.

PROTECTED AREAS IN THE PHILIPPINES

Land is declared a protected area if it is of outstanding biological importance, supporting habitats of rare and endangered species and related ecosystems. (Species are labeled "rare" if they exist in very small numbers—and are thus rarely seen—in highly specialized habitats in one or a few places in the country. Endangered species are those in danger of extinction, those that are unlikely to survive unless the causes of their disappearance are removed.) Here are some protected areas in the Philippines:

Mount Guiting-Guiting Natural Park The island of Guiting-Guiting in Sibuyan, Romblon province, has grasslands, virgin forests, and coral reefs, surrounded by a jagged shoreline. Some animal species are exclusive to the island: the Sibuyan giant moss mouse, Sibuyan pygmy fruit bat, Sibuyan striped shrew rat, and greater and lesser Sibuyan forest mouse are found nowhere else in the world. The endangered Philippine tube-nosed bat is also found in this park.

Mount Malindang Natural Park This park in Mindanao, with its waterfalls and dense virgin forests, is home to the Philippine eagle, flying lemur, long-tailed macaque, and civet cat. The ancestral land of the Subanen, an indigenous people, the Mount Malindang Natural Park is also the site of a biodiversity conservation project that involves the community in such activities as resource management, nursery establishment, and cinnamon propagation.

Mount Pulog National Park Plant life in the park includes pine and broad-leaved trees, herbaceous and woody plants, ferns, grasses, mosses, and lichens. Animal life includes the threatened Philippine brown deer, northern Luzon giant cloud rat, and Luzon pygmy fruit bat. The Ibaloi, Kankana-ey, Kalanguya, and other indigenous groups living in the area consider the mountain a sacred place.

Mount Iglit-Baco National Park This park in central Mindoro has the largest population of tamaraw (70 heads), one of the most endangered large mammals in the world and found only in the Philippines. Also found in this ASEAN Natural Heritage Site are the Mindoro imperial pigeon, black-hooded coucal, scarlet-collared flowerpecker, and bleeding heart pigeon. The human inhabitants are the Mangyan.

El Nido-Taytay Managed Resources Protected Area This area covers over 139 square miles (360 square km) of land and 208.5 square miles (540 square km) of water. Its sources of pride are its limestone cliffs, beautiful beaches, mangroves, and rolling farmlands. Five species of mammal, including the Malayan pangolin, and 16 bird species, such as the threatened Palawan peacock pheasant, Palawan hornbill, and Palawan scops owl, find their home here.

RECLAIMING METRO MANILA

Some 10 million people live in Metro Manila, competing for basic services meant to meet the needs of three to four million. Most people in Metro Manila have come from the provinces to look for the proverbial greener pastures; they are not about to go back no matter how crowded or polluted Metro Manila gets.

The metropolis faces a garbage crisis, as it becomes harder to find new landfills to dump the 4,000 tons (4 million kg) of trash collected every day. Incineration has been considered as a possible solution, but it would create another problem—toxic pollutants released into the atmosphere.

To address the problem of air pollution caused by vehicle emissions, the main source of air pollution in Metro Manila, penalties are dealt out to vehicle owners who exceed emission limits.

With less than 1 percent of the country's land area, Metro Manila has 36 percent of all registered motor vehicles and as much as 60 percent of the nation's large industries. The consequences are traffic congestion, air pollution, and solid waste disposal problems. Fortune seekers from the provinces live in slums.

Aerial view of Manila.

FILIPINOS

THE PHILIPPINE POPULATION can be divided into three groups: Christians, Muslims, and indigenous animists. These labels are religious distinctions, but they are also indicative of cultural characteristics.

More than 90 percent of Filipinos are Christians, and most are farmers and fishermen, although many also work in cities. The Tagalog live in southern and central Luzon. Visayan-speaking groups predominate in the central Philippines. Migrants from Luzon and the Visayas have established Christian settlements in Mindanao.

Muslim Filipinos, sometimes called Moro, live in Mindanao and the Sulu Archipelago. The Tausug, meaning "people of the sea current," and the Samal live by the sea, while the Maguindanao, or "people of the flood plain," and the Maranao, meaning "people of the lake," live inland.

The indigenous animists inhabit the less accessible parts of the country. They are the hardy groups of the Cordillera, such as the Ifugao and Kalinga; the shy Aeta in their mountain retreats and seaside coves; the Mindanao hill groups, such as the T'boli, distinguished by their colorful clothing, handicrafts, and rituals; and the gentle Mangyan of the island of Mindoro.

In 1971 it was reported that Stone Age hunter-gatherers had been discovered in the dense rain forests of Cotabato. Skeptics claimed the community, called Tasaday, was a hoax, although anthropologists who investigated the group confirmed its authenticity.

Above: **Filipinos of an indigenous group.**

Opposite: **A Filipina in Sinulog dance attire in Cebu.**

49

EMIGRANTS

Apart from the indigenous peoples, few Filipinos can claim pure ethnic descent. Most have inherited Chinese, Indian, Spanish, and Japanese genes from their ancestors.

A *mestiza* around the turn of the century.

The Spaniards were free to marry the Indios, though this was not encouraged among the upper classes. Chinese merchants found it convenient to have local wives who could help run their businesses, especially when dealing with local customers. (These merchants usually had families in China but were not allowed to bring them to the Philippines. The same was probably true of the Indian traders.)

The products of this ethnic mixing were the *mestizo* ("mis-TEE-so"). The *mestizo* were initially regarded with disdain or distrust, but the stigma slowly faded, as they proved themselves capable and intermarriages became more common.

THE FILIPINO DRESS

During the Spanish colonial years, upper- and middle-class Filipinos wore cotton skirts and trousers, fine jewelry, and embroidered garments made from *piña* ("PEE-nyah"), a transparent fabric woven from the leaf fibers of the pineapple plant.

For added modesty, women wore a triangular scarf-like piece across the bosom. This style of dress is called the Maria Clara, after the heroine in a popular book by José Rizal.

By blending Spanish and indigenous styles of dress, the Filipino elite made a strong fashion statement. They were a new class of Filipinos, educated and prosperous, cultured in the ways of the world. The luxurious clothing and jewelry they wore reflected their status in society and distanced them from the commoners, who were seen as "uncivilized" in their near nakedness.

Modern Filipino dress has evolved through many fashion trends: for women the European ball gown, the tassled shift of the 1920s, the shoulder pads of the 1940s, the bellbottoms of the 1960s, and the androgynous look of the 1980s; for men the three-piece suit of the 1920s, the cuffed pants of the 1940s, the leather jackets of the 1960s, and the Wall Street outfit of the 1980s. Today, traditional Philippine clothing for men includes the *barong tagalog* ("BA-rong ta-GA-log"), which is made from *piña* or from *jusi* ("HU-see") woven from banana tree fibers and worn on formal occasions. Women wear the Maria Clara on special occasions.

Filipinos perform a dance at a social function.

Metro Manila aides in their ubiquitous yellow uniforms at the Rizal Day celebration. The yellow uniform was first issued when Imelda Marcos was governor of Metro Manila, but it became the badge of support for the Corazon Aquino government.

THE POLITICS OF FASHION

Clothes, they say, make a statement, and in the Philippines this statement may be as political as it is personal. There have been times in Philippine history when Filipinos wore clothes in shame or defiance, thus giving political color to this usually apolitical aspect of culture.

When some Indios tried to imitate their colonial masters by wearing European coats with tails over tailored trousers, the Spaniards, not wanting to look like the Indios, forbade them from tucking their shirts in!

In the heady days of the "people power" revolution in 1986 Manila was a canvas of political hues: a sea of yellow-clad civilians surrounded two military camps in the capital, their yellow headbands, armbands, and hats indicating their support for Corazon Aquino; a small group clothed in green waved a banner with the name of Vice-President Salvador Laurel; the white clothes worn by the seminarians and nuns who braved the tanks; and on the other side of the city, red and blue floated below the balcony where Ferdinand and Imelda Marcos were singing their last duet on Philippine television.

THE UNBALANCED SOCIAL CLASSES

Philippine society has been described as a pyramid: the elite make up the top 2 percent of the population; the next 10 percent represents the middle class; and the impoverished masses constitute the wide base. Enclaves like Forbes Park and Dasmariñas Village, the Philippines' own versions of the United States' Beverly Hills, make it difficult to believe that there are Filipinos living in garbage dumps called smokey mountains. While some houses in Manila have gold bathroom fixtures, children of farmhands die of malnutrition. These contradictions are part of the Philippine landscape and remain a challenge for the nation's leaders.

Children from the vast dumpsite at the Smokey Mountain squatter settlement just north of Manila wait for food handouts after a church service.

Many Filipinas run businesses of their own.

THE FILIPINA

The modern Filipina ("fi-li-PEE-nah") is worlds apart from her ancient ancestor. She is the product of various cultural influences: pre-Spanish self-possession, Castilian medieval morality, American individualism, and Chinese enterprise.

The original Filipina was the priestess who healed illness, exorcised evil, and conveyed spiritual guidance to her community. After the Spanish arrival, a different morality predominated, one that "tamed" women to be demure, gentle, and pious. The effects of the Castilian era are felt even today, as modern Filipinas cling to the Maria Clara ideal.

An American education taught the Filipina that, like her male partner, she could speak her mind, could excel, could nurture ambitions. Today, women outnumber men in universities in the Philippines. They have likewise climbed their way into corporate boardrooms and made their mark in professions previously dominated by men, even running for public office and leading the nation as president.

Filipinas have contributed significantly to nation-building. In the struggle for independence, women acted as keepers of arms, couriers, and social covers for their revolutionary relatives. They took care of the wounded, fed the hungry, and sheltered the hunted.

After her husband was assassinated in 1763, Maria Josefa Gabriela Silang took over his rebellion against Spanish rule. Today, there is a network of 105 women's organizations named after this famous Filipina. Gabriela Philippines is one of the country's largest assemblies of women and works with Gabriela Network in the United States to address international women's issues.

Women constitute an important part of the labor force.

Corazon Aquino is a more recent example, a housewife who became the first woman president of the Philippines, toppling a feared dictator who had said that women were only meant for the bedroom.

The present-day Filipina performs a dual role: the traditional role of homemaker and the modern role of breadwinner. A Filipino mother continues to nurture her children and do household chores, whether she runs a multimillion-peso company or harvests rice in the fields. In return, her children are loyal to her and look on her as the greatest influence in their lives. She possesses a lot of power as the emotional center of the family. Yet she usually defers to her husband, the head of the household.

Most wealthy Filipinas either help in their husbands' businesses or pursue their own careers, some earning more than their husbands. Few educated women opt for the life of a housewife.

Yet with all the empowerment and liberation the modern Filipina enjoys, law still does not recognize her as a man's equal. For example, she cannot draw up or sign contracts without her husband's consent.

LIFESTYLE

FILIPINOS, it is said, are Malay in family, Spanish in love, and American in ambition. Three centuries of Spanish colonization and 50 years of U.S. rule have shaped a Filipino, or Pinoy ("PEE-noi"), lifestyle that combines Malay warmth, Latin charm, and American taste to produce a complex culture in which what you see may not always be what you get.

Below: **A Filipina dressed in festive gear.**

Opposite: **A northern Mindanao boy shows off his catch from the Bohol Sea off Camiguin Island.**

ATTITUDES

HIYA One of the keys to the Filipino character is the sense of *hiya* ("HEE-ya"), meaning "shame," which approximates the general Asian notion of "face" or reputation.

Hiya refers to Filipinos' concern for social conformity and suggests their deep immersion in communal tradition. It is also associated with self-esteem, something Filipinos prize above material comfort.

A Filipino's self-esteem depends on how society esteems him or her. A Filipino who is criticized in public loses social approval and consequently suffers *hiya*. This is why Filipinos react violently to public insults.

Conversely, one avoids harming another's self-esteem by never openly telling them that they are being foolish or that they smell bad. If Filipinos value their own and their neighbors' "face," they must learn *pakikisama* ("pa-KI-ki-SUM-ma"), the art of maintaining smooth interpersonal relationships, to make life easier and succeed in society.

Pakikisama
has no exact
equivalent in
English, but can
be roughly
defined as "getting
along" or
submitting to
group will.

PAKIKISAMA   This attitude prioritizes community over individual. Following the *pakikisama* guideline, a person tends to accept the majority decision rather than express disagreement with the opinion of the group.

Likewise, if a girl wants to turn down a date with her neighbor's son, rather than openly express her dislike for the boy, she will say that she has to study for an exam. This way, she avoids causing his family to lose face and helps keep relations between the two households friendly.

Filipinos dislike confrontation and are averse to breaking a congenial atmosphere with dissent. Criticism is made through a go-between or through light banter and teasing.

Pakikisama also includes a high sensitivity to social propriety, or *delicadeza* ("DE-lee-ka-DE-za"). Filipinos do not look favorably on guests who overstay their welcome, for example, or on people who take advantage of a position of power to enrich themselves.

To Filipinos, sincerity does not necessarily mean directness. The Filipino concept of sincerity includes a genuine concern for the feelings of others.

For example, when asked for a favor, they may say "yes," even if they cannot grant it, so as not to embarrass the person making the request. When invited to a social function, they may not respond if they cannot attend. They may consider the invitation to be simply a polite gesture and not binding. They want to avoid being ungracious and offending the person inviting them. In short, Filipinos regard as sincere people who try to stay true to what society expects of them.

Pakikisama has made an excellent host out of the Filipino, who will give the best food and best room in the house to a visitor, welcome or otherwise. Ironically, this hospitality was read as a sign of servility and inferiority by the early colonizers.

FILIPINO HUMOR

Filipinos have a great sense of humor, and they typically approach life in a lighthearted manner. Indeed, they have such a strong *joie de vivre* that they seem to be laughing at something all the time. There are few things Filipinos take too seriously. They poke fun at the neighbor's curtains, the latest fashion trends and movie stars, a First Lady's predilection for kitsch, and even their empty wallets.

The urge to laugh can be irrepressible in the Philippines.

Imagine a Filipino guest dressed to the nines making a grand entrance to a party. Suddenly he slips and falls flat on his face. What does he do? He stands up, smiles, and challenges the other guests: *"O, kaya ba ninyo iyan?"* ("Can you do that?")

Humor can also be political, and the Filipino people have had a lot of practice poking fun at their politicians. More than the speeches of the opposition, it was the Marcos and Benigno jokes that appealed to the people in 1986. Exposing issues became a cinch through jokes and puns: *"Marcos, ano ang problema ng bayan? Kapitalismo, Pyudalismo, Imperialismo, Ikaw mismo!"* ("Marcos, what are the problems of the country? Capitalism, Feudalism, Imperialism, Yourself!")

Estrada was a more recent target for political humorists, especially on the Internet. At one website, a visitor posted this remark: "Marcos and [Estrada] are both men who have proven something. Marcos proved that you can be very rich if you become president. [Estrada] proved that we don't need a president."

Nearly 11 million people live in Metro Manila. The vitality of this metropolis reflects its multifaceted heritage and the free-wheeling spirit of its people.

COSMOPOLITAN MANILA

Words that describe Manila emphasize its contrasts … melange, baroque, eclectic, collage, hodgepodge, potpourri.

Chinese spring rolls are dipped in vinegar and garlic, not soy sauce; 16th-century churches stand in the vicinity of skyscrapers; American pop music is used on the soundtracks of Philippine films; Chinatown *karaoke* joints play Spanish love songs.

On the road, a BMW stops beside a tricycle (the Philippine trishaw) at a red light, while street children peer into the car windows begging. Politicians meet in a coffee shop to discuss the next election.

A typhoon comes and school is suspended; movie houses make a killing. Even in the harshest of situations, Manileños know how to have a good time, constantly looking out for the best restaurant, the hottest dance club, and the trendiest fashion.

Young men brave rush-hour traffic and pickpockets to catch a basketball game on television, where they can see their favorite player make a three-point basket.

THE COUNTRYSIDE

In the *barrio* ("BA-rio"), or village, people lead communal lives, sharing daily activities from washing clothes to planting rice. Backyards run together; fences are built only to separate houses from the roads. Villagers visit the local convenience store not just to buy things but also to exchange news.

Time goes by slowly, measured not by the hour but by the season: sowing or harvesting. Nevertheless, modernity is creeping into even the most remote parts of the country.

Electrification projects bring light at the flick of a switch to more and more villages, while new telecommunication networks close gaps of distance, connecting villages to one another and to the cities and facilitating rural development.

As extending the power grid to rural areas is a costly procedure, the Philippines is advocating solar power to generate electricity in the countryside. In 2001 the government contracted with BP Solar Spain to install solar power systems in 150 remote villages in the Philippines. Led by the Philippine Department of Agrarian Reform and financed by a loan from the Spanish government, the world's largest solar energy project will cost $48 million and will benefit over 400,000 villagers, supplying homes, schools, community centers, and health clinics.

The neighborhood store is often a good place to while away the afternoon.

A fisherman's family on Simunul Island, Tawi-Tawi.

KINSHIP TIES

Of all relationships, that of the family is the most basic, the strongest, and the most enduring. The family typically consists of the father, mother, and siblings, but can extend to distant relatives as well as close friends and loyal servants. The *compadrazgo* ("COM-pud-DRAS-co") system brings non-blood relations into the family and enables the poor peasant to establish kinship ties with the richest people in the village.

The Filipino is usually not seen as an individual but as part of a family or community. Everyone belongs to a group, and the individual's identity is based on his or her kinship group. During social occasions, for instance, one tends to remain a stranger until one's kinship group is determined; interaction flows smoothly after mutual relatives, friends, classmates, colleagues, or townsfolk have been identified.

Personal independence is not of prime importance, and going it alone is simply seen as disliking one's family. Most adults who continue to live with their parents are not considered weak or childish, but devoted.

Strong kinship ties are the Filipino's best coping mechanism during critical times; they offer a strong support system that never fails to pull people through.

However, these ties are also a social bane. Corporate and political nepotism can be rationalized as being helpful to one's family. Often, Filipinos are torn between their official duties and their kinship obligations. This contradiction and duality is very much a part of Filipino identity and society.

BIRTH

Birth is usually an occasion everyone welcomes, as they speculate over the baby's gender and name and, later, which parent or uncle or aunty the baby takes after.

In rural areas, most women give birth at home. The placenta is buried beneath the house, often with an object symbolizing what the parents hope the child will grow up to be. In the cities, this practice is prohibited by the health authorities.

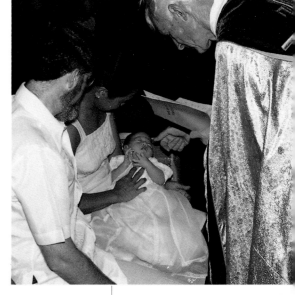

A baptismal ceremony.

The first religious ritual for a Filipino baby born into a Catholic family is baptism. For the occasion, the parents invite sponsors to be the godparents of the child. The role of the godparents is to guide and advise the child in coping in a harsh environment and to take over the upbringing of the child should the parents lose their ability to do so.

This system, called *compadrazgo,* is supposed to assure the child's social and financial future. But in reality, it is a way of networking and showing off one's influential contacts.

Children of Ilocos Norte province in Luzon.

THE GROWING-UP YEARS

Bringing up children is a communal affair in the Philippines. From the time children are born, they are handled with solicitude and tenderness by family members and friends. They are never left alone during the growing-up years, but are constantly surrounded by loved ones, if not siblings, then cousins. Filipino children are taught at an early age the value of good interpersonal relationships, and they practice it first within the family.

Filipino parents are generally unhurried and undemanding in training their children, but they are particular in nurturing concern for others and obedience. Children are essential in social gatherings, where they often sing and act for their elder relatives. Many Filipino children grow up to be good musicians, not least due to natural talent.

The onset of puberty is generally not a big occasion for celebration. Village boys prove their manhood by being circumcised without anesthesia, but boys in the cities are circumcised in a more clinical way.

DATING AND COURTSHIP

To avoid coming across as aggressive, a man has to be discreet when asking a woman out on a date. A friendly date, often in the company of friends, may be the starting point of a romantic relationship. The couple may then take the next step: going out on their own. The woman may bring a chaperon on solo dates.

A well-bred young lady in the city may show disinterest when a man woos her with flowers and chocolates and may even ignore him to test his sincerity.

In the countryside, a young man may serenade a young lady by singing beneath her window on a moonlit night.

When a couple decides they are ready, they will tell their family and friends about their romance, and then courtship begins.

A young woman being courted could find herself being serenaded by a suitor, who may bring with him a group of friends to provide the music and the camaraderie.

It is said that courting a Filipina is to court her family as well. Traditionally, a man first goes to the home of the woman he is interested in courting to introduce himself to her family, who will ask him many questions. After the first visit, he will bring gifts every time he comes again, in order to win approval from the woman's parents.

Modern courtships allow solo dates and candlelight dinners, but premarital sex is frowned on. Dating couples may go to dance clubs or rock concerts, but are expected to behave decently in public.

MARRIAGE

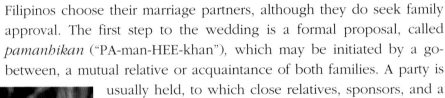

A bridesmaid at the San Agustin Church in Manila. A bride's entourage includes bridesmaids, maids-of-honor, and flower girls.

Filipinos choose their marriage partners, although they do seek family approval. The first step to the wedding is a formal proposal, called *pamanhikan* ("PA-man-HEE-khan"), which may be initiated by a go-between, a mutual relative or acquaintance of both families. A party is usually held, to which close relatives, sponsors, and a few friends are invited. The date and time of the wedding are set and church matters settled. Traditionally, the groom's family pays for the wedding.

On the wedding day, the bride and groom stand at the altar with their sponsors. The priest prays over them and they exchange rings. Following Spanish tradition, the veil sponsors place a veil over the groom's shoulders and the bride's head, indicating the union of the two families. The cord sponsors then twist a silken or floral cord in the shape of the figure eight and loosely place each loop around the bride and groom's neck, symbolizing their lifelong bond. Finally, the candle sponsors light candles on either side of the couple, a reminder of God's presence in the bond of marriage. Modern weddings include the Western tradition of the first kiss when the priest introduces them as newlyweds.

A reception follows, which in some areas includes a "money dance." Guests pin peso notes on the bride or groom in exchange for a dance, and the money the couple collects may be enough to start them out in life. The couple may also set free a pair of white doves during the reception to signify peace in their married life.

DEATH

Like birth, death is a family affair for Christian Filipinos. When there is a death, relatives and friends come to mourn with the bereaved, who welcome visitors with food and drink and tell them of the circumstances of the death. A wake is often a reunion of seldom-seen relatives and friends, who keep night vigils with the bereaved family. Immediate family living overseas return, lending joy to a sad occasion.

While sending wreaths is customary, most people feel that giving money is more practical as it helps defray the cost of the funeral service. After the burial, overt grief is expected of the family. A husband or wife will cry or even faint at a spouse's burial.

The dead are always remembered in the Philippines. Nine days of prayers are held for the deceased after the burial, and death anniversaries are celebrated with a Mass or a visit to the grave.

Most Filipinos bury their dead in Christian cemeteries. All Saints Day is a special day for families to visit their family graves.

RELIGION

THE ANCIENT PEOPLE of the Philippines believed that the world was ruled by powerful spirits manifested in nature. They believed that these spirits could bring either happiness and good fortune or disease and death. They also believed that the god Bathala created heaven and earth and reigned supreme over the sea and river gods, the god of death, and other gods.

There are Filipinos who still worship rocks, trees, and animals and perform rituals to ask the rain god for water or the earth god for a bountiful harvest. While they can pray directly to the gods, they believe that their prayers will be heard more easily if they go through a priestess.

There are also Filipinos who revere the spirits of their dead relatives, offering sacrifices to ask for guidance and protection.

For generations one of the rites of passage for young boys of the Ifugao group in the northern region was carving from hardwood the image of the rice god, a central god in their culture.

Each family placed a pair of wooden rice god figures outside their home to watch over their granary. During ceremonial rituals, Ifugao elders poured the sacrificial blood of chickens over the images, praying for a good harvest.

Today, Ifugao artisans practice their woodcarving tradition not so much to revere the rice god as to earn money from selling the images.

Below: **A painting of an ancient priestess.**

Opposite: **A festival at the Quiapo Church in Manila.**

FOLK CHRISTIANITY

The Spanish missionaries arrived filled with a zealous desire to save the animist souls of the indigenous people. The missionaries built impressive churches and preached the virtuous path to salvation.

But the indigenous people found that medieval Castilian philosophy did not fit into their worldview, so they went on practicing animism behind the backs of the priests. The Spaniards may have imposed Christianity, but it would be inaccurate to say that the indigenous people fully accepted the foreign religion. Historians seem to see not the Christianizing of a people, but of their animistic practices. Christianity in the Philippines is really a unique folk variety, incorporating animistic beliefs.

One can easily recognize this in the practice of Christianity in the Philippines. For example, Filipinos have a strong devotion to the Virgin Mary and the Child Jesus. They acknowledge the Virgin Mary in many different capacities: as a shield against foreign invasion, as a protector during travel, and even as a fertility goddess. Filipino children often call her Mama Mary.

There are also cults devoted solely to the Child Jesus. Worshipers bathe images of the Santo Niño, or Holy Child. They clothe the statues in rich brocade, treating the Child Jesus as a princely guest in their homes. More than 50 icons of the Virgin Mary and the Child Jesus in the Philippines are said to be miraculous.

Another example of folk Christianity in the Philippines is the veneration of saints for prayers answered: for a good harvest, for rain, for the right spouse, for children.

Early Filipino converts may have seen features of their own rituals in Catholic sacraments. They may, for example, have associated the sacrament of baptism with their own healing rituals, which also used the symbolism of water.

The Spanish friar may have simply replaced the indigenous priestess as spiritual mediator. While the missionaries tried to completely destroy indigenous symbols and practices such as slavery and polygamy, some of the European Catholic practices they introduced blended with indigenous ritual practices. For example, they acted out biblical stories to teach the indigenous people about Christianity. Filipinos today act out the passion of Christ during Holy Week.

A faithful people, Filipinos look to religion for strength in times of trouble and attribute their accomplishments to divine guidance. What is important to them is that someone or something more powerful than themselves turns the wheel of life and may be counted on for help.

Above: **A Santo Niño statue.**

Opposite: **A priest administers Holy Communion to a tribal girl.**

71

CATHOLIC PRACTICES

Like their fellow believers around the world, Catholics in the Philippines celebrate several sacraments that they believe are sources of spiritual life. Baptism is the first sacrament, celebrated soon after birth. First Holy Communion and Confirmation come when the child is older; they strengthen the believer's bond with God.

The sacrament of Holy Matrimony often marks the transition to responsible adulthood. The final sacrament, the Anointing of the Sick, is administered to people who are very ill and on the brink of death.

Catholics pray as a community at Masses, novenas, and processions. In the family, they recite the rosary and say grace before meals. On Holy

Religious processions are a common event in the Philippines.

Thursday, worshipers visit churches; on Lenten Fridays, they abstain from eating meat; on Christmas Eve, they attend midnight Mass. When Catholics move to another house, they invite a priest to bless their new home before they settle in.

A mosque in downtown Manila. In the mid-16th century, Manila was a Muslim city-state until the arrival of the Spaniards. Muslims today form the largest minority in the Philippines.

OTHER FAITHS

The Philippines, Asia's only Christian nation, is 83 percent Catholic and 9 percent Evangelical Christian.

Although Islam reached the Philippines before Christianity, it was contained by colonization. Filipino Muslims make up 6 percent of the population and live mostly in southern Mindanao.

The remaining 2 percent of the population profess other faiths. Taoism and Buddhism flourish in the countless Chinese communities. Hindus and Sikhs form a small minority and have their own religious enclaves.

Even a humble chapel occupies an important place in a Filipino community.

CHURCHES

Almost every *barangay* has a church or chapel. In some parts of Manila and in most of the countryside, churches date back to the 16th or 17th century, products of the religious zeal of missionaries and the ingenuity and artistry of indigenous craftsmen. These churches were built solidly, to withstand typhoons and fires, but unfortunately did not always survive earthquakes. San Agustin, for example, has been severely damaged by several earthquakes.

A typical church has a squarish nave and a bell tower, and the priest's residence is located beside or behind the church. The bell tower was traditionally a measure of the church's prosperity—the taller it was, the wealthier its congregation. But more important, the bell serves to announce baptisms or weddings and to call the community to Mass.

Inside the church, there is a central altar with a crucifix and shrines on the sides with the statues of saints.

FAITH HEALING

Faith healing—curing sickness without the aid of implements or drugs—was practiced in the Philippines especially before the advent of medical science. It was the domain of the *babaylan* ("BA-BY-lun"), or priestess, and later the herb doctor. Modernization did not eliminate faith healing.

Filipinos who cannot afford to go to a hospital or clinic still turn to faith healers, who normally do not charge for their service for fear of losing their gift. Some faith healers claim to be guided by Catholic saints and may even have medical knowledge.

One form of faith healing is prayer—healers exorcise spirits of disease. Healers may also cure by touch, simply laying their hands on the sick person or using herbal concoctions and oils.

Most faith healers cure while in a trance. The most dramatic, most controversial form of faith healing is psychic surgery. The healer, using just the hands, opens up the body of the sick person and extracts a tumor or any diseased part. No anesthesia is used because apparently no pain is felt.

Herbal medicines range from the leaves, bark, and twigs of trees to oils culled from indigenous plants. Herb doctors use these natural medicines to cure all forms of ailments.

Reports of successful operations have raised intense debate. Medical doctors who remain unconvinced claim it is all a sham, that the psychic surgeon conceals in his hand a bloodied cotton ball and the extracted tissue is actually the liver of a chicken or pig.

On the other hand, there are the patients who testify to the power of psychic healing. Is it possible that spiritual power can open and close the body without pain or blood? Shaman or sham, the faith healer will remain "open for business" so long as people believe.

BELIEF IN MIRACLES

The mysticism surrounding many Catholic festivals in the Philippines reflects a strong belief in miracles. From a young age, Filipino children hear stories about apparitions of the Virgin Mary and religious icons that weep or bleed. While for believers, these supernatural phenomena form the basis of "miracle faith," skeptics call it superstition.

In 1948 Teresita Castillo, a Carmelite novice in Lipa city in Batangas province, was reported to have seen an apparition of the Virgin Mary standing on a cloud, dressed in white, a golden rosary in her hand. According to Teresita, she received the vision 19 times and the apparition asked for penance and prayer to be offered for the clergy.

There were also accounts of hundreds of rose petals falling from the sky, each bearing a different holy image, such as the Virgin Mary holding a crucifix, the Last Supper, the Holy Family, and the crucified Jesus with three women at the foot of the cross. In 1991 there were reports of crosses of light appearing on frosted glass panels. Reports of crosses of light were first heard in 1988 in California and later in Seattle, Canada, and Washington, D.C., before showing up in the Philippines.

ANCIENT AMULETS

The *anting-anting* ("UN-ting-UN-ting") are ancient amulets or talismans, passed down through a bloodline from one generation to the next. They may come in the form of a bracelet, necklace, or ring, and their owners may wear it like a medal. Each has a unique design, and many consist of spell-like inscriptions on pieces of cloth, bark, or paper.

No shaman alive today knows for sure how the first *anting-anting* came into existence. It is said they were created in dark times when evil creatures roamed the islands. The *anting-anting* empowered the wearer to fight evil and protect the weak. In pre-Spanish times, every village had shamans, many known for their ability to make the *anting-anting*.

The *anting-anting* were said to give the wearer different powers—spiritual, physical, and psychic—and to protect them against bullets and poisonous snakes. There have been instances in the past when soldiers, thinking the *anting-anting* could make them invincible, rushed unarmed toward the enemies' guns, with fatal consequences.

It was also alleged that if a sick person possessed an amulet, he would not die until he bequeathed the amulet to a younger relative. There were supposedly even talismans that could make a person fall in love with the wearer. Owners of the *anting-anting* had to perform certain rituals at specific times to preserve the magical powers of the talismans.

Filipinos today use talismans or amulets mainly for good luck in their businesses and for protection from accidents and natural disasters. There are stalls in Quiapo, Manila, selling talismans, which the vendors claim have powers to help people in business, relationships, and sickness.

However, these modern-day lucky charms are not the same as the *anting-anting* of old that were supposed to give the wearer supernatural powers.

Above: **An example of the *anting-anting*.**

Opposite: **Devotees use towels to touch the face or hands of the image of Jesus during the Black Nazarene procession. The towels are later used to anoint the sick.**

FOLK BELIEFS

Early Filipinos believed in a soul and life after death. The indigenous groups have preserved this ancient belief. The Bagobo of southeastern Mindanao believe in the existence of two souls within each individual, one good and one evil. The Bukidnon believe that there are seven souls within a person, and these souls merge and migrate to Mount Balatocan after death. Most acknowledge the possibility of spirits coming back to earth; they have invented prayers and rituals to lead spirits to the afterlife.

Christianity reinforced belief in the afterlife, and indigenous rituals incorporated Christian elements, such as a cross or holy water used to subdue pagan creatures of the underworld.

Christianity has not been able to stem folk beliefs in fairies, elves, and other unseen beings. Filipinos often say *"Tabi tabi po"* ("TA-bi TA-bi po") to excuse themselves for fear of stepping on elves. A pregnant woman is never left alone so no hungry spirit, or *asuang* ("AS-wahng"), can eat her baby. If a child suddenly falls ill, the parents suspect an earth spirit is the culprit.

Such beliefs and behaviors show that Filipinos recognize worlds other than their own and that they are willing to straddle the fence between logic and mystery.

MYTHS AND LEGENDS

People create myths in order to make sense of things and events in the world that cannot be otherwise explained. Based on their worldview and environment, early Filipinos tried to answer the question of where they came from by weaving creation legends.

One legend about the origin of the Filipinos goes like this: between heaven and earth blew a sea wind and a land wind. The winds married and brought forth a reed or bamboo. A bird pecked at the bamboo, breaking it in two, and from the bamboo emerged Silalak, the first man, and Sibabay, the first woman. They married and gave birth to the first Filipinos.

A version of the legend says that Silalak and Sibabay were siblings, forced to mate in order to propagate the human race. Another version says the woman and the man emerged from separate bamboos and had no knowledge of each other before they met, married, and bore children.

The belief that the bird is the creature who unlocked human life suggests an ancient reverence for birds. The Tagalog identify their chief god, Bathala, in a blue bird.

A northern Luzon legend explains that the sky used to be low, but a maiden pounded her rice so vigorously that her wooden pole pushed the sky high. On the clouds she hung her jewelry, and they twinkled as stars.

Legends also help shape ideals, as in the legend of Maria ng Makiling, the beautiful goddess who inspired José Rizal with the purity of her love, even for a lesser mortal. Maria had the power to either unite people in love or separate them if they were unworthy of each other. She fell in love with a mortal man who was in love with a mortal woman. Maria was heartbroken, but she gave the couple her blessings anyway, and she never revealed her beautiful self to mortal eyes again.

Above: **Figurines of the Filipino Adam and Eve.**

Opposite: **A folk Christian holds an icon of the Child Jesus.**

LANGUAGE

MORE THAN 100 LANGUAGES are spoken in the Philippines. The eight major ones are Tagalog, Cebuano, Ilocano, Bicolano, Kapampangan, Pangasinan, Hiligaynon, and Samarnon. Tagalog is also spoken by Filipinos living in the United States, Canada, the United Kingdom, Saudi Arabia, and elsewhere. Philippine languages belong to the Malayo-Polynesian family; each has dialects specific to towns or *barrios* in the city or municipality where the language is concentrated.

English is an official language in the Philippines, but the national language is Filipino, which is based on Tagalog and other languages. Filipino is spoken in the Metro Manila area and in the southern Luzon Tagalog provinces. It is understood by 90 percent of the population and is the language of instruction in many schools. The government intends to make Filipino the language of administration nationwide.

Left: **A movie billboard in English and Filipino.**

Opposite: **A man makes a call from a Philippine Long Distance Telephone Company booth.**

81

Many newspapers and magazines are in either Filipino or English.

FOREIGN LANGUAGES

It is no surprise English is the most widely used foreign language in the Philippines; it has been the language of instruction in schools throughout the country for almost eight decades. It is still the language of instruction in universities and the medium of government and mass communication. English serves as a bridge language among Filipinos who speak different regional languages and is spoken throughout the country, especially in business negotiations.

The Philippines is the third largest English-speaking nation in the world, following the United States and India. Filipinos speak a variety of

English culled mainly from the United States and infused with the idiosyncrasies of local languages and dialects. In informal situations, Filipinos often use a combination of languages, creating a hybrid called Taglish (Tagalog-English).

Before 1987, Spanish was a required subject in school. Spanish speakers are now rare in the Philippines, although most Filipinos have a working knowledge of the language. The national language is liberally laced with Spanish words.

Hokkien or Fujianese is mostly spoken by the Chinese and has contributed significantly to the vocabulary of Philippine languages. Indian influences can be seen in ancient scripts.

A MIXED BAG OF NAMES

Many Filipinos bear Iberian-sounding surnames without having Iberian ancestry. This is because of a 19th-century Spanish decree that required all Filipinos to use a Spanish surname.

In fact, in many Philippine towns, the people bear last names starting with the same letter of the alphabet. The Spaniards allocated surnames by town, reserving surnames starting with the letter 'A' for people in the capital. The outlying towns received surnames starting with subsequent letters: 'B' in the second town, 'C' in the third, and so on. This made it easy to identify a person and trace his or her municipal origins.

The choice of first names was dictated by a person's birth date. A Filipino couple was likely to name their baby after the saint whose feast day it was on the child's birthday.

Some women have the name Maria, abbreviated as Ma., before their name, as a sign of respect for the Virgin Mary.

Tagalog speakers, the second largest linguistic and cultural group in the Philippines, number at least 10 million, and are located in central Luzon (including Manila) and parts of Mindanao.

The *mano* and *beso-beso*.

BODY TALK

TOUCHING Filipinos are a "touchy" people in that relatives and close friends make a lot of physical contact in greeting and in conversation. A young Filipino greets an older person with a gesture of respect called *mano* ("MAHN-no"), or "hand." The young person puts the back of the older person's hand on his or her forehead.

Relatives and friends generally do a cheek-to-cheek greeting called *beso-beso* ("BAE-so BAE-so"), or "kiss-kiss." However, people of the opposite sex prefer to shake hands when meeting for the first time, especially at business meetings and social occasions, and the man is expected to wait for the woman to extend her hand.

EYEBROW HELLO Filipinos may say hello without words, but with an upward nod of the head and a quick lift of the eyebrows. If the eyebrow "flash" lingers too long, it signifies a query.

GESTURES OF HOSTILITY Staring suggests provocation and may endanger the curious. Standing arms akimbo signifies arrogance, except in a teacher reprimanding a student or a policeman confiscating a driver's license.

GESTURES OF RESPECT Filipinos may greet their superiors with a nod. When walking between two people in conversation, one says, "Excuse me" and bows, extending the hand in front.

To get someone's attention, one does not shout or point a finger. Filipinos make eye contact and signal with a nod or with the hand, palm facing down.

The versatile smile of the Philippines.

SMILE Filipinos do everything with a smile—they praise with a smile, criticize with a smile, condole with a smile, take life's trials with a smile. A confrontation is best avoided, but if it is necessary, a smile is the best way to start. An embarrassing moment is covered with a smile, while allegations are dismissed with a knowing grin.

ARTS

ANCIENT PHILIPPINE LITERATURE consisted of myths, legends, songs, riddles, proverbs, epics, and tales that touched daily life. Folk songs depicted the lifestyles of the indigenous groups and their hopes and aspirations. Some invented work songs, such as the rowing song of the Tagalog and the rice-pounding song of the Kalinga. The Ilocano composed war songs, love songs, and death chants. The Cebuano and Bontoc sang dirges and lamentations, recalling the deeds of the deceased.

Epics and tales explained the creation of the world, the landscape, and animals. The epics of the Maranao and Ifugao often revolved around supernatural events.

When the Spaniards colonized the archipelago, they brought religion-based morality and passion plays and stories based on the lives of the saints. By the 18th and 19th centuries, however, a group of educated Filipinos had emerged. They began writing novels, poems, and other forms of literature in Spanish, as well as in the vernacular. Intellectuals who studied in Europe penned anti-Spanish, anti-clergy texts, not with a Filipino audience in mind, but a Spanish one.

Francisco Baltazar, known by his pen name, Balagtas, wrote allegorical poetry to depict the injustices of the Spaniards in the Philippines. Balagtas' most famous piece was *Florante at Laura*. The greatest works of the period, and perhaps in all of Philippine literary history, were the novels of José Rizal. Rizal's best-known works were *Noli Me Tangere* and *El Filibusterismo*, both depicting the abuses of the Spaniards and the nationalistic aspirations of the Filipinos.

Above: **José Rizal's acclaimed novel *Noli Me Tangere*.**

Opposite: **A folk theater performance.**

87

LITERATURE IN ENGLISH AND FILIPINO

Barely 20 years after American missionaries set up the first English class in the islands, Filipinos began writing stories in this foreign language.

The 1950s and early 1960s were the golden age of Philippine literature in English, with writers like Francisco Arcellana, Bienvenido Santos, and the most famous, Nick Joaquín.

With the surge of nationalism in the 1960s and 1970s, many writers shifted to Filipino as a medium, and the regional languages were given due importance. Social realism became the main literary style.

Filipinos today are big fans of popular culture. While many may like Shakespeare, they also love comics. *Sari-sari* stores often rent comic books so patrons can follow their favorite series.

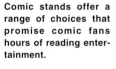

Comic stands offer a range of choices that promise comic fans hours of reading entertainment.

DANCE

Philippine dance reflects Malay and Spanish influences. The *singkil* ("SING-kil") performed by a graceful Filipina between bamboo poles never fails to entertain audiences. The *jota* ("HO-ta") and *curacha* ("coo-RA-cha") of Spain are the highlight of school programs and fiestas. Indigenous dances imitate nature, for instance, the movement of birds. The famous bamboo dance, the *tinikling* ("ti-NI-kling"), mimics the agile movements of a bird as it traipses along reeds. There are also dances to celebrate a courtship or a warrior's victory or to mourn death.

Filipinos love to dance, whether at a village festival, at a club on a Saturday night, or in the living room at home. Hardly anywhere else in the world can television viewers watch so many dance performances and contests as in the Philippines. The Cultural Center of the Philippines in Manila is the national hub for ballet performances.

The *singkil,* a folk dance of Muslim origin.

MUSIC

Music is a part of everyday life in the Philippines. Filipinos sing in the bathroom, in the kitchen, even in the office. They hum a melody when stuck in traffic. Children learn to play the guitar, piano, violin, or other musical instrument from an early age, and the more gifted go on to participate in international music festivals and competitions.

Contemporary Philippine music may be Western in sound, yet it remains Filipino at heart in its sentimentality, romantic content, and mellow mood. Although many songs originally written in English have been translated into Philippine languages, listeners are increasingly choosing to listen to original local compositions, especially those in the Filipino language.

Freddie Aguilar, one of the Philippines' best-known folk singers, in concert.

An indigenous Filipino plays a traditional musical instrument.

Clubs in the Philippines play folk, jazz, rock-and-roll, and other kinds of music. Concerts and live acts are frequent. The Philippine Philharmonic Orchestra performs at the Cultural Center in Manila and in other big cities around the country. Filipinos in Manila can enjoy free open-air concerts at Rizal Park on Sundays and Paco Park on Fridays.

Filipino musicians also perform in other parts of Asia and elsewhere on the international scene. Regine Velásquez was voted Favorite Artist for the Philippines at the 2002 MTV Asia Awards, where she sang a duet with American pop star Mandy Moore.

Another Filipina who has made it big with her singing (and acting) talent is Lea Salonga, who at the tender age of 17 landed the lead role in the musical *Miss Saigon*, for which she won a Tony for Best Actress. Salonga was also in the Broadway show of *Les Misérables*, as Eponine.

Ethnic music lives on in the indigenous communities. Traditional instruments include a harp called the *kubing* ("KHU-bing"), a gong called the *kulintangan* ("KHU-lin-THA-ngan"), and a bamboo nose flute. The International Bamboo Organ festival held in the Philippines every year attracts participants from other parts of the world as well. While there are Filipinos who want to preserve ethnic music in its pure state, there are also those who wish to incorporate it into contemporary music.

The *tuba,* a Western import, is played during fiestas and on public holidays.

The *cenaculo* is staged in many villages and towns during Holy Week.

DRAMA AND THEATER

Early Philippine drama was performed as part of rituals observed at major stages of life such as birth and death as well as in work activities such as planting and harvesting. Like early literature, early drama was enmeshed in everyday life, without stage, lights, or camera.

European drama came with the Christian evangelists. The *cenáculo* ("si-NAH-KU-loh") emerged as a distinctly Philippine version of the passion play. The musical operetta called the *zarzuela* ("sahr-SWHE-lah") has today evolved into other forms of contemporary theater.

Dramas in English were first performed in the universities on topics such as historical events and domestic problems. In the late 1960s, with the resurgence of nationalism, writers began using Filipino, and drama was seen as the most potent art form for exposing national issues.

Present-day theater in Filipino has reached high standards, even as plays in English continue to be written and performed by university student groups and professional theater troupes.

PAINTING AND FILM

Painting in the early Spanish years was reserved for religious purposes. Secular paintings increased in the 19th century, serving as souvenirs for foreign visitors. These paintings showed the indigenous people in their traditional dress. Damián Domingo y Gabor (circa 1790–1832) was the best-known painter in this genre. He set up the country's first fine arts school. In 1884 Juan Novicio Luna and Felix Resurreción Hidalgo won awards in Spain and Paris for their paintings.

More recent noted painters include César Legaspi (1917–94) and Vicente Manansala (1910–81).

Filipino films face intense competition at the local box office. Filipino viewers throng the theaters to watch Hollywood films, but the response to homegrown films is lukewarm. Nevertheless, local film companies are working to improve the quality of their products in various genres such as drama, comedy, action, and horror. There are directors who focus on creating films that not only tackle the realities of Philippine life, but also bring out the best in Philippine cinematic artistry.

Films that address serious social issues can often provoke controversy. In 2001, *Live Show*, a documentary film directed by José Javier Reyes, was banned by the government for its "pornographic" portrayal of sex workers. Over 300 filmmakers, actors, and students in Manila protested the ban. Screened at film festivals in the United States, Europe, and Australia, *Live Show* earned acclaim for depicting the poverty that forces Filipino men and women into the sex industry.

A portrait of a lady by Juan Luna, who won the most prestigious international art award of the time, the Prix de Rome.

TRADITIONAL CRAFTS

Many indigenous communities have their own handweaving traditions, using different natural materials to produce textiles with a variety of colors and designs.

The T'boli weave dyed tree bark strands into geometric designs. Yakan weaves are a spectrum of color. Filipinos from the Panay islands and Mindanao use silk or the fibers of the pineapple and abaca. Weavers in Ilocos Sur create checked and striped patterns, while those in Abra base their designs on the images of their gods.

While many weave as part of a tradition passed on from generation to generation, for some the craft is simply a source of income to support their families. They can earn money from the sale of their products to tourists.

However, there is a real concern that the art of handweaving is becoming extinct. The younger generations do not have an interest in learning their parents' craft. Local governments are thus seeking to revive traditional weaving by encouraging handweaving in schools. Other ways used to promote the art include displaying handwoven cloth in trade shows and using it to design fashionable clothing.

Woodcarving and furniture-making have produced the most intricate crafts from trees.

For Paete in Laguna, woodcarving is a town industry, while the town of Betis in Pampanga has the highest reputation for wooden furniture.

Basketry is very developed among indigenous communities in the Mountain province, Mindanao, and Palawan.

Traditionally, woven baskets are used by their makers to catch fish or store grain or other goods, yet these baskets adorn the houses of the wealthy because of the skill and artistry they exhibit. A Philippine basket may be made from one material or a combination such as bamboo and rattan, depending on the province or town its maker comes from.

Other crafts the Philippines is famous for are the shellcraft of Cebu and the silver filigree of Baguio.

The Community Crafts Association of the Philippines (CCAP) is a non-profit organization in Quezon city that serves over 2,000 artisans from all over the archipelago. Founded in 1973, the CCAP aims to improve the social conditions of Filipinos living in villages and slums by providing them with assistance in marketing their traditional crafts.

Baskets in all shapes and sizes.

LEISURE

FILIPINO CHILDREN HAVE FEW TOYS but many playmates. For many children in the Philippines, toys are a luxury. As they are usually surrounded by relatives and friends, their play activities tend to involve a lot of games and social interaction. They go to the backyard or the street and indulge in an hour of *luksong-tinik* ("look-SONG-tee-nik"), in which a player jumps over a stick or over the outstretched arms of playmates;

sungka ("song-KAH"), in which players collect shells or stones in their "home" hole in a specially-made wooden board; *siklot* ("SEEK-loot"), similar to jacks; *sipa* ("SEE-pah"), in which players kick a palm or paper ball; as well as hide-and-seek, blind man's buff, and kite flying.

Adults play chess, bingo, or *mahjong* ("mah-JONG"), a game of Chinese origin.

No fiesta is complete without special games such as cracking-the-pot, in which blindfolded players try to hit a hanging pot using a pole; trying to hook a ring while riding a bicycle; stepping on one another's shoulders to reach reward money at the top of a greased bamboo pole; and sack racing.

Animal competitions are also popular. Carabao races and horse fights are held in some parts of the country, but the most popular animal sport is cockfighting.

COCKFIGHTING

Cockfighting is a centuries-old bloodsport, popular since the times of ancient Persia, Greece, and Rome. It is still practiced in Asia and South America. In the Philippines, cockfighting is virtually a religion, and matches are a weekly "duty." Well-heeled businessmen and dirt-poor peasants fill the galleries of cockpits on Sunday afternoons, playing a game of chance with plumed warriors. Cockfight aficionados will beg or borrow to bet on their favorite birds. Owners (*above*) groom their prized possessions, massaging and exercising the birds.

Finger-play precedes the actual match. A *kristo* ("KRIS-toh") stands in the center of the pit, taking bets. Without paper or calculator, he is somehow able to accurately match bets with faces. He moves around with arms outstretched and fingers extended, signaling to the gamblers which bird is receiving bets at any particular moment. The gamblers point any number of fingers up, down, or sideways to signal their bets.

Then the match begins; the trained birds, equipped with sharp spurs, or gaffs, claw at each other in a battle to the death. The contest ends when one bird runs away or dies. The winning bird must seal his victory by pecking at the loser twice.

SPORTS

Sports and recreational activities in the Philippines vary according to terrain. Filipinos engage in outdoor sports like tennis, jogging, baseball, volleyball, track and field, soccer, and golf. Bowling, pelota, boxing, and weightlifting are popular indoor alternatives.

The highlands beckon to mountain climbers and hang-gliders, while the coasts draw swimmers, scuba-divers, and windsurfers. But the islands' grand passion is basketball, with the Philippine Basketball Association (PBA) driving the sport's popularity for more than 25 years.

Above: **Weightlifting at the CCP Complex in Manila.**

Below: **Windsurfers at Boracay Island resorts.**

BASKETBALL

Basketball is the national obsession in the Philippines. If there is anything aside from politics that Filipinos from different generations— or even different genders— can fight about, it is basketball.

The basketball court is as common as the jeepney; no town plaza or college campus is without a court. Children create single-basket courts (*right*) in street corners, or a flower pot in the backyard will do just fine. While height does matter on the court, the lack of it does not seem to stop the smaller-built from venturing into the sport by making up for their disadvantage with speed.

Televised championship games attract millions of viewers, who watch with anticipation as their favorite teams battle for supremacy. To fans, PBA teams are the

object of admiration and loyalty. On a championship night everything comes to a standstill as energies focus on the game. After an exhausting finish fans of the winning team celebrate, while those of the defeated team sigh in dismay, foreseeing the ribbing to come the next day.

With names such as Coca-Cola Tigers and FedEx Express, teams in the PBA are attractive product movers, and businesses pour huge amounts of advertising money into the games.

FUN IN THE TOWNS AND VILLAGES

Entertainment and recreation in the countryside coincide with the seasons. During the hot summer months, young people look forward to picnics. When the rains come, they amuse themselves with the radio.

As soon as they are able, children go out into the streets to play. In most *barrio*, roads are an extension of the house. On moonlit nights, children play hide-and-seek and other local games.

Religious holidays are other occasions that provide a break from work in the fields. The most anticipated event is the patron saint feast day, the reason for the town fiesta.

When the fiesta is imminent, the carnival comes to town. Complete with rides, dice games, shooting, and ring booths, the carnival entertains the townspeople for a month or so, building up festive tension until the feast day arrives.

The celebration climaxes with brass bands roaming the streets from dawn to dusk, sumptuous family meals at home, and the Mass and procession.

THE TOWN FIESTA

There is no tradition more Philippine than a fiesta. The town fiesta is a celebration of the pact between the people and their patron saint, an offer of thanksgiving to the saint for his or her protection over the community. The fiesta is also a time of baptisms, weddings, and family reunions.

During the fiesta, homes are open to everyone, including strangers, and the occasion shows Filipinos at their most hospitable. Carnivals, games, and beauty contests give the residents a chance to release the pent-up energy and stress from a year of toil.

A fiesta needs preparation. People spruce up their homes, cook special food, and pray for nine days. Preparations reach fever pitch as the feast day draws near, the air electric with anticipation.

On the day itself, people wear their Sunday best. Visitors are advised to eat only a small amount of food in the first house they visit because that is certainly not going to be the last. Wine and goodwill flow freely.

The carabao fiesta is celebrated in farming towns on the feast day of San Isidro in May. Farmers parade their groomed and decorated carabao around town. Then comes the carabao race, after which the beasts are guided to kneel (*above*), as the priest blesses them. The seaside town of Pandan in Antique celebrates its fiesta in April in honor of Saint Vincent Ferrer. Pandan holds an annual boat-rowing competition during the fiesta.

FUN IN THE CITY

The cities offer cosmopolitan pleasures such as shopping in mega malls, dining in luxurious restaurants, and enjoying movies in cinema complexes. Karaoke lounges dare anyone gutsy enough to take the microphone, while dance clubs are great places for Filipinos to indulge in their passion for dancing. Philippine television broadcasts a host of variety shows and soap operas for the housebound.

Museums offer a leisurely form of education. The National Museum in Manila and the Ayala Museum in Makati give visitors a good introduction to Philippine history and culture.

Music lounges are popular nightspots.

Rizal Park, Manila. The park—an oasis of gardens, lagoons, fountains, and playgrounds—also houses the National Library, and an aquarium and planetarium.

PLACES TO GO

For newcomers, the Philippines offers interesting historical sites that provide a crash course on local history and culture. In Manila, there is Fort Santiago, a mute testament to colonial oppression; Casa Manila, a replica of the Spanish stone house, or *bahay na bato* ("bah-AY na ba-TO"); the Monument at Rizal Park; and relics of contemporary history such as the EDSA marker and the Malacañang Palace museum, where one can enter Imelda Marcos' boudoir.

Outside Manila, there is the Rizal family house in Laguna, the Barosoain church in Bulacan, the Aguinaldo house in Cavite, the Magellan shrine in Cebu, and MacArthur's landing spot in Leyte.

If one wants a bird's-eye view of the different regional cultures, one goes to Nayong Pilipino, which contains replicas of important Philippine historical and scenic spots. Paco Park, one of the most pleasant nature spots in Manila, is the site of evening cultural-musical presentations featuring local and international talents.

NATURE TRIPS

Nature has blessed the Philippines with abundance as well as beauty. The weary soul can take refuge in any of the beautiful beaches around the country. Boracay in the Visayas is famous for stretches of white sand and a relatively isolated location.

Batangas, Mindoro, and Pangasinan are great for those who have just a few days to spare. El Nido in Palawan is famous for its underwater treasures. Pagsanjan in Laguna is noted for waterfalls and boatmen who deftly negotiate dangerous rapids.

Volcanic springs are popular tourist spots. Baguio is a favorite refuge during the hot months, the air cool and invigorating. Banaue, a mountain village farther north, presents a life as simple as it was centuries ago and a glorious morning view of the famous rice terraces.

Pagsanjan Falls, two hours south of Manila, offers the memorable boating adventure of shooting the rapids in a hair-raising run down-stream to the calm waters below.

FESTIVALS

THERE ARE FIVE RELIGIOUS EVENTS celebrated nationwide in the Philippines: Holy Thursday, Good Friday, and Easter in March/April; All Saints' Day on November 1; and Christmas on December 25.

LENT

Lent, the biggest religious season in the country, commemorates the death and resurrection of Jesus Christ. Although the season culminates in the joyous celebration of new life at Easter, the mood throughout Lent is somber in reflective anticipation of Christ's death and crucifixion. A blaze of color and dramatic festivals, however, lightens the atmosphere. The season of Lent begins with Ash Wednesday when priests draw a cross of ash on the foreheads of Catholic worshipers.

Left: **Palm leaves are brought to church to be blessed on Palm Sunday. The leaves remind of the triumphant entry of Jesus Christ into Jerusalem before He was crucified —the event that ushers in the Holy Week.**

Opposite: **A creative capacity for enjoyment is an innate part of the spirit of the Filipinos.**

HOLY WEEK

The climax of Lent is Holy Week, which commemorates the week of Christ's death and resurrection. Palm Sunday ushers in Holy Week. In memory of Christ's entry to Jerusalem, people bring palm fronds to the church service to be blessed by the priest.

The folk aspect of Philippine Christianity is seen in a ritual called *pabasa* ("pa-BA-sa"), when the teachings of Christ are chanted. Flagellants beat their bare backs with glass-spiked leather thongs, not as an act of masochism, but in fulfilment of a *panata* ("pa-NA-ta"), or vow. The devotee lives up to a promise to undergo the pain and humiliation of this penitential act in exchange for a granted request or a forgiven wrong. Some *pabasa* participants even go to the extent of having themselves tied or nailed to a cross on Good Friday.

An air of gloom descends on Good Friday. At mid-afternoon, the last words of Christ are spoken and explained in the pulpits. In the evening, a replica of Christ's bier is taken around the town in a procession.

At Easter dawn, the meeting of the risen Christ and the Virgin Mary is reenacted. Two carriages, one carrying a figure of the risen Christ and the other a figure of the grieving Mary, are taken to opposite parts of town. They are to meet at a selected church, where children dressed as angels sing as they lift the mourning veil from the statue of the Virgin Mary. The two carriages are then brought into the church amid the joyous ringing of bells.

CHRISTMAS

Christmas in the Philippines begins as early as late October. Carols play over the radio, and classrooms, offices, and homes put on festive cheer with tinsel and ribbons, Christmas trees and lights.

At home, a replica of the Nativity scene complete with shepherds and kings is set up. By the window hangs a lantern, either in a riot of color or in the shape of a star.

Nine dawn Masses precede Christmas Day; rice cakes eaten after each Mass make rising early a little less difficult. On Christmas Eve, the family gathers to eat a sumptuous meal after midnight Mass. On Christmas morning, the children wake up to gifts from Santa Claus.

In a Bulacan town, Mary and Joseph's search for a place to stay just before the birth of their son is reenacted. The actors are turned away at every house they visit, finally finding shelter in a church.

A giant lantern lights up San Fernando town in Pampanga province on Christmas Eve. It is here that the most spectacular lantern festival is held.

HONORING SAINTS

Almost all *barangay* and towns hold fiestas, but some fiestas are more famous than others.

In Manila, the best-known fiesta is the feast of the Nazarene, patron saint of the capital's oldest—and central—district, Quiapo. In January, thousands of devotees clog the main roads of Quiapo in a body-to-body procession. Leading the procession are male devotees called *hijo* ("EE-ho"), or sons, who pull a carriage bearing a figure of Nuestro Padre Señor Jesús Nazareno (Our Father, Jesus of Nazareth).

The figure of the Nazarene has allegedly been blackened by the constant libation of indigenous perfumes. Devotees have to push their way through a crowd in order to reach the figure and wipe a cloth or handkerchief on the face or hands of the icon; the devotees then use the "blessed" cloth or handkerchief to wipe themselves, following an ancient folk ritual.

Outside Manila, the most colorful fiesta is celebrated in May in Lucban, Quezon. This is the feast day of San Isidro de Labrador, the patron saint of farmers. Called the *pahiyas* ("pa-hee-yahs"), this fiesta is a thanksgiving for a good harvest, which is reflected in the food-based decorations that color the town during this fiesta.

The townspeople make thin, leaf-shaped wafers from pounded rice dyed pink, yellow, and other bright colors. These wafers, or *kiping* ("kee-ping"), are then used to make lanterns, flowers, and other hanging pieces to adorn windows, doors, and walls together with fruit, grains, and vegetables.

Towns situated near rivers celebrate their feast days with water parades. Icons mounted on water carriages are paraded along rivers rather than along streets. Devotees ride decorated *banca* ("bun-ka") or immerse themselves in the river. Some riverside towns celebrate with water throwing, reminiscent of the world-famous Songkran water festival in Thailand.

Filipinos in Calumpit in Bulacan province throw water on one another on the feast day of John the Baptist, Calumpit's patron saint. There is also a water parade that features pagodas and brass bands. Manila, the Camiguin Islands, and various cities across the country also celebrate the feast of John the Baptist with water parades, processions, and boat races.

The village of Aliaga in Nueva Ecija celebrates the feast of John the Baptist with even more folk tradition. During the Taong Putik (Mud People) Festival, devotees visit people's homes, dressed in dry banana or coconut leaves and smeared with mud. At each home, they are given candles or gifts to be offered to the saint. The "mud people" then gather at the village church and give thanks to the saint for blessings received. An outdoor Mass follows, after which devotees carry an icon of the saint out of the church and into the streets.

Above: **Woven palm hats and *kiping* clustered like giant translucent petals in various shades of pink, yellow, and green hang outside a house as offerings to San Isidro de Labrador, the patron saint of farmers.**

Opposite: **Devotees escort the Nazarene in Quaipo.**

FOLK FESTIVALS

Many folk festivals retain strong elements of animist religions, while incorporating Christian figures.

The Ati-Atihan of Kalibo in Aklan province is a local Mardi Gras held in honor of the Santo Niño. Revelers, their faces blackened with soot, go around town to the beat of drums and rhythmic shouts of "*Hala bira!*" The procession snakes along the narrow streets of Kalibo. Women holding Santo Niño icons rub elbows with hedonists drunk on the heart-pounding beat of the mountain peoples.

May is the month of the Virgin Mary. Flores de Mayo, a flower festival in honor of the Virgin Mary, lasts through May. During this time, girls in the rural areas offer flowers in churches. Dressed in all their finery, the girls walk under flower arches amid candles and lights.

In the cities, however, the Flores de Mayo has virtually become a fashion show, and the designer gowns worn by the girls attract more attention than the devotions.

The month of flower offerings culminates with the Santacruzan, a one-day celebration in which the Empress Helena's search for the Holy Cross is reenacted. The Santacruzan is a parade of biblical characters and allegorical figures.

The traditional procession features the empress with her son, Constantine the Great, as well as biblical characters. Adorned icons of the Virgin Mary are paraded through streets lined with bamboo poles from which hang bundles of coins and bread, candies, and fruit.

Bacoor in Cavite province, where fishing is a major occupation, holds a fisherman's festival in May that features a boat procession. People praying for miracles and blessings wave leafy branches in the path of the pagoda-like boats to the sounds of a brass band and splashing water.

Bocaue, a town in Bulacan province, holds a river procession—the Pagoda-sa-Wawa festival—in July to commemorate the finding of a crucifix in the Bocaue River by an ancestor. A large replica of the historic Holy Cross of Wawa is paraded on a barge, followed by a fleet of fishing boats.

The Kadayawan is a five-day celebration originating among Davao's indigenous groups such as the Bagobo, Maranaw, and Mandaya. The festival is held in August in thanksgiving for a plentiful harvest. *Kadayawan* comes from an indigenous word meaning "anything that is good."

The Kadayawan has become an extravagant event, with street dancing, a parade of floral floats, concerts, contests, exhibits of indigenous arts and customs, and fireworks displays. For Davaoeños, the festival's significance runs deep, a celebration of their ethnic roots in thanking God for blessings received.

Above: **The *Santacruzan*.**

Opposite: **Christian and pagan elements come together at the Ati-Atihan with the Santo Niño.**

A Muslim girl dances at an Islamic celebration on Simunul Island in Tawi-Tawi province.

OTHER FESTIVALS

Chinese Filipinos set off their firecrackers to celebrate the Lunar New Year, the traditional Spring Festival. In the Philippines, a land with no spring, the Chinese give their friends *tikoy* ("tee-coy"), or glutinous rice cake, prepare red packets of money for children of friends and relatives, and invite lion dancers to their stores to ensure a new year of prosperity.

In southern Mindanao, Muslims celebrate Hari Raya Puasa, the birth of Muhammad, and Ramadan.

The Shrine of Valor on top of Mount Samat in Bataan province, central Luzon—a memorial to the dead of World War II.

OFFICIAL HOLIDAYS

January 1	New Year's Day
April 9	Bataan Day
May 1	Labor Day
June 12	Independence Day
December 30	Rizal Day

January 1, a nonreligious holiday, is always considered part of Christmas. The New Year is greeted with firecrackers and fireworks exactly at midnight, after which a lavish meal is shared. April 9 commemorates the bleakest time in Philippine history, when the combined American-Filipino forces were forced to surrender to the Japanese after a valiant last stand. June 12, 1898, was the first time the Filipinos declared their independence from a colonizer. This was made possible by the death of a great man, José Rizal, on December 30, 1896.

FOOD

THE STAPLE FOOD of the Philippines is rice, the main agricultural crop. Fish harvested from the country's long shoreline complements rice in the Filipino's basic meal. The traditional meal combines ingredients derived from the immediate surroundings, and cooking methods are simple. Fish and meat can be stewed with string beans, radishes, and soured tamarind or indigenous lemon.

Coconut and sugar are abundant and thus form a major part of the Philippine diet. Coconut milk is used to cook fish, meat, or vegetables, while its flesh can be candied or mixed in fruit salads. Filipinos have developed an incorrigible sweet tooth. A meal is never complete without dessert, the sweeter the better.

In comparison with the spicy food of Southeast Asia, Philippine food is sometimes bland, but it is perfect for the sensitive palate. Filipinos do, however, like their food a little salty.

Left: **The Philippine seas yield a rich harvest of seafood.**

Opposite: **Diners at this waterfall buffet can enjoy a sumptuous meal while cool water flows over their feet.**

Heart of palm spring rolls, or *lumpiang ubod* ("loom-piang OH-bood"). The Filipinos didn't just adapt Chinese dishes; they renamed them.

A MIXED TABLE

Philippine cuisine is as mixed as Filipino ancestry. The national diet includes many dishes of foreign origin, often adapted to suit the Filipino palate. Many indigenous foods have in turn been influenced by the cooking styles of the Malay immigrants, the Chinese traders, and the Western colonizers.

The Spanish component in the Philippine diet is strongest. From Spain, the Philippines inherited dishes such as *morcon* ("MOR-kon"), beef stuffed with pork fat; *pochero* ("put-CHAY-roh"), beef, chicken, and pork chunks stewed with cabbage, green beans, and Spanish sausage; and that great culinary delight called *paella* ("pah-AY-lah"), a combo of rice, seafood, and meat.

From the Chinese came all sorts of noodles, or *pancit* ("PAHN-sit"). Filipinos have localized Chinese noodle dishes, creating hybrids such as *pancit palabok* ("PAH-lah-book") and *pancit malabon* ("MAH-lah-bon"). Other Chinese foods popular in the Philippines are rice porridge, meat buns, spring rolls, and pastries filled with red beans or lotus seeds.

The Americans introduced refrigerators and ovens as well as salads, pies, hamburgers, and canned food. Italian spaghetti, sweetened for Filipino tastebuds, is considered party fare.

Most indigenous concoctions come in the form of *kakanin* ("KAH-kah-nin"), a variety of rice cakes. Some dishes are distinctly national: *adobo* ("ah-DO-boh"), a dark stew of chicken and pork; *dinuguan* ("DEE-noo-gwan"), stew cooked in pig's blood; *bagoong* ("BAH-goong"), a shrimp paste with an off-putting smell; and *balut* ("BAH-lut"), boiled duck's egg with a half-formed chick. The latter two are formidable for those who have not acquired the taste, and eating them is considered the ultimate test of a foreigner's adjustment to Philippine life.

Halo-halo, meaning "mix-mix," is a typical dessert made with shaved ice, beans, gelatin, milk, and whatever else the maker can put into a tall sundae glass.

CHICKEN *ADOBO*

1 teaspoon salt
1 teaspoon ground black pepper
$^1/_2$ teaspoon ground paprika
2 $^1/_4$ pounds (1 kg) chicken pieces
2 bay leaves
12 cloves of garlic, finely chopped

$^2/_3$ cup (158 ml) vinegar or lime juice
$^2/_3$ cup water
3 teaspoons oil
1 quartered and skinned tomato
2 sprigs of coriander leaves

Mix salt, pepper, and paprika. Turn chicken pieces in the mixture. Place the chicken in a pan with bay leaves and garlic. Add vinegar or lime juice and water to the chicken. Slowly bring to a boil, then simmer, turning the chicken pieces until tender. Remove the cooked chicken pieces to drain; set aside the liquid in the pan. Heat oil in another pan and fry the chicken pieces until golden brown. Arrange the fried chicken pieces on a serving plate and pour the liquid in the pan over the chicken. Garnish with tomato quarters and coriander. Serve with rice and soy sauce.

RICE

The first thing Filipino children learn in the kitchen is how to cook rice. They wash the grain in a pot and fill the pot with water up to the second joint of the middle finger. Then they set the pot over low heat. They learn when to turn off the heat—not too early, not too late—and how long to leave the rice to steam before serving.

Suman is one of many Philippine rice treats.

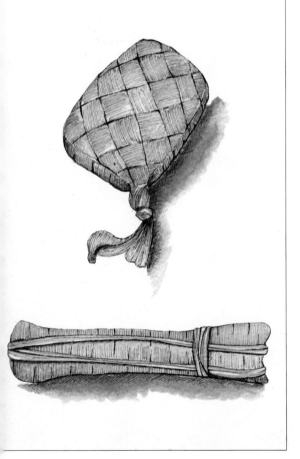

Rice served as a staple is usually boiled or fried; for special occasions, rice is cooked in different ways. Glutinous rice is baked to make a hundred kinds of *kakanin* ("KAH-kah-nin"). The most popular rice cake at Christmas is *bibingka* ("bi-BING-kah"), which is rice with coconut, egg, and milk baked in a clay oven.

Almost every province has its own *suman* ("SOO-mahn"), wrapped in coconut or banana leaf. The wrapper is a work of art that adds to the fragrance of the filling. The *pandan* ("PAHN-dun") leaf of the pandanus plant, a screw pine, is often used when steaming rice and making desserts. The leaf gives food a special fragrance, flavor, and color.

Rice mixed with cocoa is a child's favorite snack, usually eaten with something salty like dried fish. Ground rice is a necessary ingredient in other rice-based dishes such as steamed rice cakes, rice balls in sweet coconut milk, and rice cooked in sugar.

Palitaw ("PAH-lee-tao") is a rice cake eaten with grated coconut and aniseeds. Rice gruel is generally fed to the sick; it may also be combined with chicken or tripe to make an enjoyable meal.

EATING RITUALS

For Filipinos, food not only feeds the body but the soul as well. Eating is a ritual that allows one to touch base with family and friends. There is hardly an occasion when food is not served. A casual neighborly visit can bring out a tray of spring rolls or a plate of noodles. Shopping, watching a basketball game on television, or even keeping vigil at a wake are all opportunities to share food.

Most Filipinos eat with a fork and a spoon. However, certain foods are best eaten using the fingers—fried rice and dried fish.

It is normal for Filipinos to share their food with others. If the person sitting next to you on the bus opens a bag of potato chips, he or she will offer you some. House guests are always served food and drinks, and if they come unannounced in the middle of a meal, they will be asked to join in. It would probably be uncomfortable for the host if he or she had not cooked anything special that day, so the guests may considerately decline. But they will oblige if the host insists so as not to hurt his or her feelings.

Philippine hospitality ensures that guests are always served first.

121

WHERE TO EAT

Restaurants in Manila serve food from many cultures—Italian, French, Spanish, Indian, Thai, Vietnamese—to satisfy the healthy Filipino appetite. While in the past eating out was a novel chance to experience foreign tastes, today indigenous fare has taken on its own glamor with the introduction of elegant restaurants serving indigenous food. Tourists are attracted to the exotic ambience of such places; some restaurants even encourage their customers to eat using their fingers! Wooden or wicker plates lined with banana leaves and coconut juice served in the coconut shell add to the novelty.

The ice-cream man with his very recognizable cart of flavors.

If it is regional fare one craves, then fancy restaurants are not the place to go, according to food critics. Instead, it is the roadside stalls patronized by jeepney drivers and manual laborers that serve the most authentic regional fare.

Of course, patrons at roadside stalls do not enjoy the kind of service and atmosphere that cafés and restaurants offer. At roadside stalls, the customer chooses from an array of dishes behind a glass compartment, and the vendor piles the portions on a plate for the customer to take to a table and eat. Cart hawkers sell hot noodles and porridge at very low prices. Cola comes in bottles or may be poured into a plastic bag with a straw inserted.

In the market areas, competition is so stiff that vendors employ criers to cajole—maybe even force—customers to buy from their stalls. Sitting between two fierce criers can be quite an uncomfortable experience.

DESSERT ANYTIME

To satisfy their sweet tooth, Filipinos have concocted a variety of puddings, cakes, cookies, candies, flans, and other desserts. Here is a mouthwatering selection:

- *bibingka*—glutinous rice cakes with a variety of toppings: fresh grated coconut, coconut cream, corn kernels, cottage cheese, white cheese, cheese strips, melted cheese,...
- *ginatan* ("GHEE-na-tahn")—yam, sweet potato, and banana in coconut milk
- *halo-halo* ("HA-lo-HA-lo")—beans, sago, banana, yam, and gelatin in crushed ice and milk
- *leche flan* ("LET-che flahn")—baked egg custard
- *mais con hielo* ("MAH-ees kon YEH-lo")—sweet corn kernels in crushed ice and milk
- *maruya* ("MAH-ro-yah")—banana slices dipped in a batter of flour, egg, milk, and butter, then deep fried and rolled in sugar
- *pastillas de leche* ("pas-TEE-liahs deh LET-cheh")—candied carabao milk
- *sorbetes* ("SOR-veh-tehs")—local ice cream
- *suman* ("SOO-mahn")—rice cake wrapped in coconut or banana leaf
- *ube* ("OO-beh")—yam with milk
- *yema* ("YEH-mah")—candy made from egg yolk and milk

And in case there is a shortage of homemade desserts, different kinds of fruit preserves and jams from the supermarket are stocked in the kitchen cabinet.

NO TIME TO EAT

To Filipinos, eating is a serious matter, and time is taken to savor meals. But with the fast pace of urban life, quick meals are often the way to go. The roadside stalls are perhaps the cheapest and most convenient places to get one's daily meals. And of course there is fast food—not only the original Western import, but local versions as well.

Fast-food outlets are found in every shopping mall, ready to feed hungry shoppers in a jiffy. Besides the established American chains such as McDonald's, there is the successful homegrown chain Jollibee. Fast-food stores even deliver, so people need not step out of their homes and offices for lunch or dinner. The delivery person brings ordered lunches into the office, and there are "back-ups" for other employees who have no time to wait in line at a cafeteria but have not placed orders with the restaurant in advance.

FIESTA FOOD

The fiesta is not just a social and religious event; it is also a culinary celebration. The fiesta table is a grand feast. It may feature such homey dishes as *dinuguan* or the sour soup *sinigang* ("SI-nee-gahng"), but with something extra to make it special for the occasion.

If there is one word that describes fiesta food, it is "rich." Pork leg *estofado* ("es-tuh-FAH-do") is simmered in burned sugar sauce and thickened with the nectar of ripe banana. An *embotido* ("em-bo-TEE-do") is a steamed roll stuffed with egg, olives, relish, and ground meat. *Galantina* ("gah-lahn-TEE-nah") is shredded or diced chicken flavored

Lechon is fiesta fare at its finest. It is usually grilled on a spit over an open fire.

with broth, milk, and spices. *Lumpiang ubod* is a spring roll filled with shrimp, pork, heart of palm, and only the softest coconut pith. The roll is sometimes topped with gravy seasoned with ground garlic. The *lapu-lapu* ("LAH-po LAH-po") fish is steamed, then garnished with mayonnaise, relish, peas, corn, parsley, and shredded carrots.

The centerpiece of the fiesta spread is *lechón* ("LET-son"), a whole, four-month-old roasted pig with crunchy golden skin. Filipinos in Luzon eat *lechón* with a thick liver sauce; those in the Visayas prefer vinegar mixed with soy sauce and crushed chili.

No fiesta party is complete without dessert. *Leche flan*, or egg custard, is made with duck's eggs for a creamy effect and drowned in burned sugar sauce. Gelatins in all colors, filled with raisins or tiny pieces of fresh fruit, are topped with whipped cream or milk. Soft and fluffy coconut strips are cooked with *pandan* leaves to create an aromatic preserve called *macapuno* ("MAH-kah-POO-no").

An eclectic Manila cuisine: *paella*, spring rolls, raw fish vinaigrette, crabs in coconut milk, and fancy fruit juices.

125

Stalls such as this can be found in all parts of the Philippines, a tropical fruit paradise.

FRUIT

Philippine fruit is mostly tropical. The most common are watermelon, papaya, avocado, soursop, jackfruit, mango, pineapple, guava, indigenous orange, and several varieties of banana. Some fruit is seasonal, such as rambutan and *siniguela* ("si-nee-GWE-la"), a green berry; some fruit is regional, for example, strawberries grow only in the cool highlands of the Mountain province, while Mindanao is the exclusive domain of the mangosteen and durian.

Fruit is eaten mostly as a dessert or snack, but it also has medicinal and superstitious value. For example: papaya is a cure for constipation, while banana is a good source of dietary fiber; guava can cause appendicitis and *siniguela* can cause diarrhea. Expectant mothers crave green mango, but they stay away from *duhat* ("DO-haht"), a black cherry, believing that it will give the baby a dark complexion.

KITCHEN UTENSILS

The traditional Philippine kitchen is equipped with an earthen pot, a bamboo dipper, and a Chinese wok. It is believed that rice is best cooked in an earthen pot; the pores in the clay are said to preserve the flavor of the rice. Water is stored in a large clay jar. Older Filipinos swear that water from the jar is sweeter and fresher than water from the tap.

Ingredients used to make rice cakes are pounded in a heavy stone grinder. The *sandok* ("SUN-dok"), made of half a coconut shell tied to a stick, is the indigenous ladle. The *kawali* ("kah-WALL-ih"), the Chinese wok, is used for frying. A bigger version, the *kawa* ("KAH-wah"), is used at fiesta time in order to cook enough for the large party. Food is prepared on a bamboo table or on a *paminggalan* ("PAH-ming-gah-lahn") where plates and glasses are left to dry.

Traditional kitchen equipment is not convenient for the fast pace of urban life. Modern technology has made the preparation of everyday meals a snap. The seconds-to-minutes microwave oven has replaced the gas stove, and the electric blender the cumbersome stone grinder.

Above: **Molds with fish, bird, and other designs are used to shape little pastries.**

Left: **The *kawali* and *sandok* are still in demand despite the availability of modern appliances.**

OF FILIPINOS AND SPIRITS

When Magellan set out to fight that upstart of a chieftain, Lapu-Lapu, he and his men had just been to a feast where they drank a sweetish liquid that put them in high spirits. Strangely, before the day was over, Magellan and his men were defeated.

The drink that Magellan had was *tuba* ("TOO-bah"). It is still drunk today, a wine made from the sap of an unopened coconut bud. The tip of the bud is lopped off, and the sap is left to flow for a whole day. Tree bark is mixed with the sap, giving it a reddish hue.

Lambanog ("lahm-buh-noog") is a powerful, clear distilled liquid that burns as it goes down the gullet. It is made from coconut fermented in a bottle with chewing gum and apples or raisins for a month. *Tuba* and *lambanog* are popular in coconut-producing provinces such as Laguna, Batangas, and Quezon.

Up north, the Ilocano ferment sugarcane sap in huge jars buried under their houses. The product is a wine called *basi* ("bah-see"). The Bontoc and Ifugao make rice wine called *tapuy* ("TAH-pui").

Not to be outdone by the West, Filipinos have concocted their own beer, the internationally acknowledged San Miguel brand. There are also a few Philippine brands of rum, such as Manila Dark Rum and Tanduay Rum. The latter has won international renown and is one of the world's best-selling brands of rum.

Trust a Filipino to find a place and time for a couple of drinks. In the spirit of camaraderie, a group of men share a bottle of liquor on a street corner. Each takes a shot, called a *tagay* ("TAH-gai"). Refusing a *tagay* embarrasses the person offering the drink, and this may lead to a brawl. Women in the countryside can gulp down a glassful of liquor without batting an eyelash; some can even outdrink their male counterparts.

Above: **The sap of the coconut is collected in bamboo containers fastened to the tree. Sap gatherers move between trees by way of connecting bamboo poles.**

Opposite: **Sharing laughs over drinks.**

PAELLA

This recipe serves 10 to 12.

1 pound (454 g) chicken, cut into pieces
1/2 pound (227 g) pork, cut into pieces
Salt and pepper
Vegetable oil
1 pound large shrimp, boiled
12 clams
2 garlic cloves, minced
2 tablespoons olive oil
1 medium-sized onion, sliced

3 cups (710 ml) roasted rice
3 cups chicken stock
1/2 cup (118 ml) tomato ketchup
1/2 cup water
1 piece Italian sausage, cooked and sliced
6 whole raw squid, cleaned
1 cup (237 ml) green peas
1 red pepper, sliced

Season chicken and pork with salt and pepper. Pan-fry in vegetable oil over medium heat until cooked, then set aside. Season shrimp with salt and pepper, then set aside. Boil clams until shell opens, then remove top and set aside. Fry garlic in olive oil until brown. Add onion, roasted rice, chicken stock, tomato ketchup, and water. Cover and bring to a boil. Reduce heat until the liquid evaporates and the rice is cooked. Garnish with remaining ingredients. Cover and simmer for 10 to 15 min.

KUTSINTA (STEAMED BROWN RICE CAKE)

1 cup (237 ml) rice flour
2 cups (473 ml) brown sugar
3 cups (710 ml) water

A few drops red and yellow food coloring (to give cakes a brownish tinge)
Freshly grated coconut

Combine rice flour, brown sugar, water, and food coloring in a bowl and mix well. Pour mixture into muffin pans, half full. Place pans in a steamer filled with water 2 inches (5 cm) deep. Cover and cook for 30 minutes. Add more water in the steamer if necessary. To check if cakes are cooked, stick a toothpick in one; the pick should come out clean. Leave to cool, then remove cakes from the pans. Top with freshly grated coconut (*below center*).

PALITAW (BOILED WHITE RICE CAKE)

1 cup (237 ml) glutinous rice flour
³/₄ cup (177 ml) water

White sugar
Freshly grated coconut

Mix rice flour with water to make a dough. Roll bits of the dough into balls and flatten. Boil water in a saucepan. Carefully release the flattened dough balls into the boiling water. Remove the cakes when they float. Leave to cool, then roll in sugar and freshly grated coconut (*below left*).

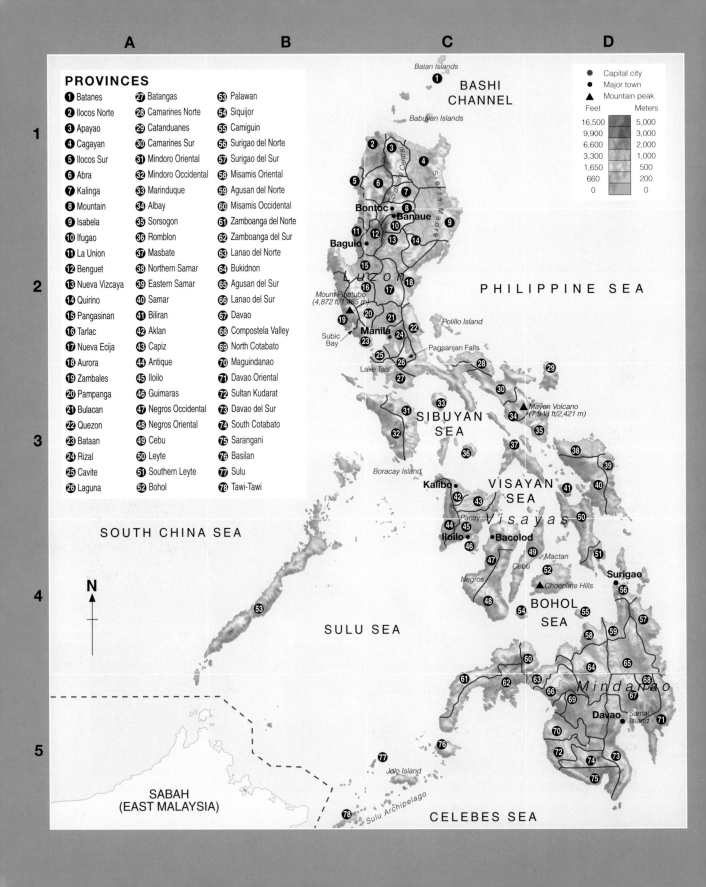

PROVINCES

1 Batanes
2 Ilocos Norte
3 Apayao
4 Cagayan
5 Ilocos Sur
6 Abra
7 Kalinga
8 Mountain
9 Isabela
10 Ifugao
11 La Union
12 Benguet
13 Nueva Vizcaya
14 Quirino
15 Pangasinan
16 Tarlac
17 Nueva Ecija
18 Aurora
19 Zambales
20 Pampanga
21 Bulacan
22 Quezon
23 Bataan
24 Rizal
25 Cavite
26 Laguna

27 Batangas
28 Camarines Norte
29 Catanduanes
30 Camarines Sur
31 Mindoro Oriental
32 Mindoro Occidental
33 Marinduque
34 Albay
35 Sorsogon
36 Romblon
37 Masbate
38 Northern Samar
39 Eastern Samar
40 Samar
41 Biliran
42 Aklan
43 Capiz
44 Antique
45 Iloilo
46 Guimaras
47 Negros Occidental
48 Negros Oriental
49 Cebu
50 Leyte
51 Southern Leyte
52 Bohol

53 Palawan
54 Siquijor
55 Camiguin
56 Surigao del Norte
57 Surigao del Sur
58 Misamis Oriental
59 Agusan del Norte
60 Misamis Occidental
61 Zamboanga del Norte
62 Zamboanga del Sur
63 Lanao del Norte
64 Bukidnon
65 Agusan del Sur
66 Lanao del Sur
67 Davao
68 Compostela Valley
69 North Cotabato
70 Maguindanao
71 Davao Oriental
72 Sultan Kudarat
73 Davao del Sur
74 South Cotabato
75 Sarangani
76 Basilan
77 Sulu
78 Tawi-Tawi

Capital city
Major town
Mountain peak

Feet	Meters
16,500	5,000
9,900	3,000
6,600	2,000
3,300	1,000
1,650	500
660	200
0	0

BASHI CHANNEL

Batan Islands

Babuyan Islands

Sierra Madre

Cordillera Central

Bontoc
Banaue
Baguio

Luzon

Mount Pinatubo
(4,872 ft/1,485 m)

Manila

Subic Bay

Lake Taal

Pagsanjan Falls

Polillo Island

PHILIPPINE SEA

Mayon Volcano
(7,943 ft/2,421 m)

SIBUYAN SEA

Kalibo

Boracay Island

VISAYAN SEA

Visayas

Panay

Iloilo
Bacolod

Negros

Mactan

Cebu

Chocolate Hills

Surigao

BOHOL SEA

Samal Island

Davao

Mindanao

SOUTH CHINA SEA

N

SULU SEA

Palawan

SABAH
(EAST MALAYSIA)

Jolo Island

Sulu Archipelago

CELEBES SEA

MAP OF THE PHILIPPINES

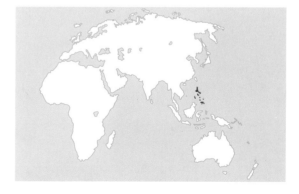

ECONOMIC PHILIPPINES

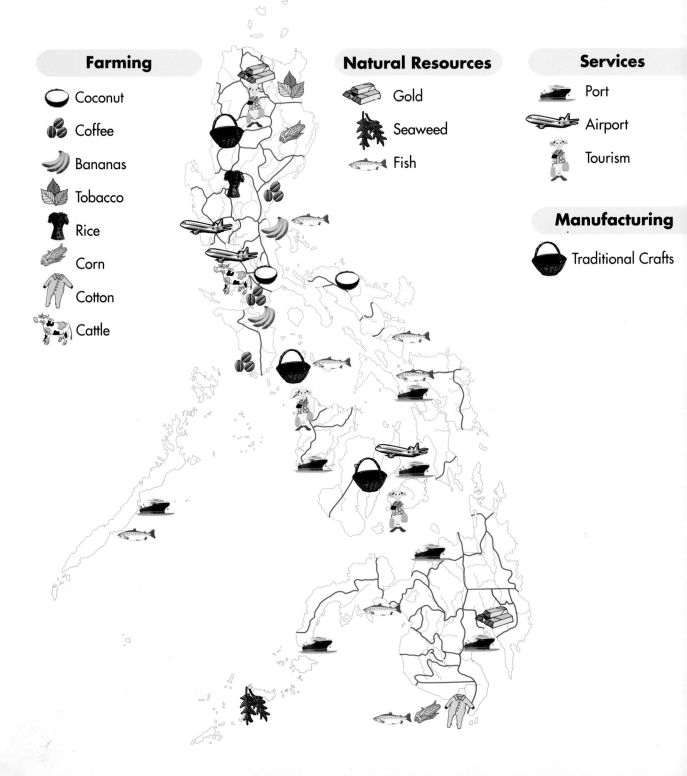

Farming
- Coconut
- Coffee
- Bananas
- Tobacco
- Rice
- Corn
- Cotton
- Cattle

Natural Resources
- Gold
- Seaweed
- Fish

Services
- Port
- Airport
- Tourism

Manufacturing
- Traditional Crafts

ABOUT THE ECONOMY

OVERVIEW

The Philippine economy is based on agriculture, light industry, and supporting services. In 1998 Philippine farming suffered poor weather, and the economy shrank due to the Asian financial crisis. From a negative 0.5 percent growth rate in 1998, the economy bounced back with about 3 percent growth in 1999. Reforms to help the Philippine economy include deregulation and privatization and revising taxation.

GROSS DOMESTIC PRODUCT

$310 billion (2000)

MAIN INDUSTRIES

Textiles, pharmaceuticals, chemicals, wood products, food processing, electronics assembly, petroleum refining, and fishing

AGRICULTURAL PRODUCTS

Bananas, beef, coconuts, corn, eggs, fish, mangos, pineapples, pork, and sugarcane

CURRENCY

1 Philippine peso = 100 sentimos
Notes: 10, 20, 50, 100, 500, 1000 pesos
Coins: 5, 10, 25 sentimos; 1, 5 pesos
1 USD = 53.50 pesos (July 2001)

IMPORTS

$35 billion (2000)

MAIN IMPORTS

Mineral fuels, lubricants, and related materials; electrical apparatus and appliances; machinery; base metals; and textile yarns

EXPORTS

$38 billion (2000)

MAIN EXPORTS

Semiconductors and electronic microcircuits, finished electrical machinery, garments, crude coconut oil, and gold

LABOR FORCE

48.1 million (2000)

UNEMPLOYMENT

10.1 percent (July 2001)

INFLATION

5.4 percent (October 2001)

TRADING PARTNERS

United States, Japan, South Korea, Singapore, Taiwan, Hong Kong, and United Kingdom

REGIONAL/INTERNATIONAL COOPERATION

The Philippines is a member of the World Trade Organization, Asia Pacific Economic Conference, and Association of Southeast Asian Nations.

CULTURAL PHILIPPINES

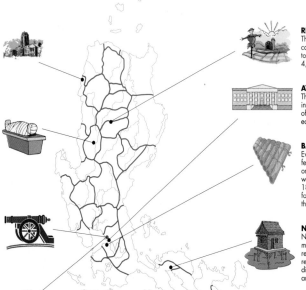

ANCESTRAL HOUSES
Vigan is home to 193 ancestral houses and historic buildings built in the late 1800s and early 1900s. The brick-and-plaster houses, with their red tiled roofs, grand doorways and staircases, broad floorboards, and sliding windows, display the ingenuity of indigenous craftsmen, who created a style suited to the demands of an earthquake-prone location.

KABAYAN MUMMIES
The mummified bodies of Ibaloi royalty were found in caves around Kabayan in the early 1990s. It is believed the mummies were made between A.D. 1200 and 1500. Animal-shaped coffins and artifacts such as pottery and clothing have also been discovered in the caves. It is likely that the Spanish arrival put a stop to the practice of mummification.

INTRAMUROS
Manila's walled city is where Legaspi erected a fortress in 1571. Within lies Fort Santiago, housing the cell of José Rizal before his execution by the Spanish and a marble cross marking the grave of 600 Filipinos and Americans killed by the Japanese in World War II. Also here is Manila's oldest fort and its Byzantine circular stone maze.

MALACANANG PALACE
The Palace has stood on the northern bank of the Pasig River as a symbol of power for three centuries. Once the official residence of the Spanish governor-general and later of the American civil governor, the Palace became the official residence of the Philippine president in 1935.

MORIONES FESTIVAL
This festival takes place in Marinduque during Holy Week. Participants wear painted papier mâché masks and dress up as biblical figures. They reenact the story of a Roman centurion who converted to Christianity and was beheaded. The story goes that when he pierced the side of Jesus Christ, the blood touched and healed his blind eye.

TABON CAVES
This system of 29 caves in Quezon is known as the cradle of Philippine civilization. The caves hid the secrets of the earliest Filipinos until 1962, when a team discovered the 22,000-year-old fossils of the Tabon Man.

RICE TERRACES
The spectacular rice terraces around Banaue were carved out of the hillside by Ifugao cultivators 2,000 to 3,000 years ago. The terraces, some reaching 4,920 feet (1,500m), stretch like steps to the sky.

AYALA MUSEUM
This museum in Makati City promotes awareness and interest in Philippine culture and history through exhibits of historical artifacts and contemporary art and educational programs and publications.

BAMBOO ORGAN FESTIVAL
Every February, Las Piñas holds a week-long music festival revolving around an old 1,031-pipe bamboo organ 13 feet (4 m) in height and width. The organ was first built in the early 1800s and rebuilt after the 1896 revolution. In the 1970s, it was sent to Germany for restoration, then returned to Las Piñas. So began the annual festival.

NAYONG PILIPINO
Nayong Pilipino in Pasay City is the Philippines in miniature. The theme park highlights the country's regions and cultures. Museums exhibit the furniture, religious symbols, arts, and other belongings of the different ethnic groups. Gardens, an aquarium, and an aviary feature indigenous fish, bird, and plant life.

ATI-ATIHAN FESTIVAL
Held every January in Kalibo, the Ati-Atihan reminds the visitor of Mardi Gras. Celebrants dressed in bright costumes, faces painted with black soot, dance in lively processions and parades.

CHOCOLATE HILLS
More than 1,000 mysterious cone-shaped hills dot the land for miles in Bohol. The slopes of the hills are green in the rainy season, but turn a chocolate brown in summer when the grass dries.

WINDSURFERS' PARADISE
Boracay is the country's best-known windsurfing destination. With a large reef-rimmed lagoon, the island boasts windspeeds in the range of 10–30 miles per hour (18.5–55.6 km per hour) from December to April. The annual Boracay International Funboard Cup brings together sailors from around the world for six days of races and parties.

ABOUT THE CULTURE

OFFICIAL NAME
Republic of the Philippines

FLAG
The national flag of the Philippines consists of a blue band on top, a red band at the bottom, and a white triangle based on the hoist edge. The center of the triangle features a yellow sun with eight rays representing the eight provinces that fought for independence from Spain. In each corner of the triangle is a yellow star representing one of the three main island groups.

NATIONAL ANTHEM
Lupang Hinirang ("LOO-pahng hee-NEE-rahng") —Ordained Land

CAPITAL
Manila

MAJOR CITIES
Manila, Quezon, Davao, Cebu, and Baguio

MAIN ISLAND GROUPS
Luzon, Mindanao, and the Visayas

LITERACY RATE
94.6 percent (1995)

POPULATION
76.5 million (2000)
Luzon, the largest island group, is home to more than half the total population. Metro Manila has a population of some 10 million people.

ETHNIC GROUPS (A SELECTION)
Apayao, Bagobo, Bontoc, Boholano, Cebuano, Ifugao, Ilocano, Kalinga, Mandaya, Manobo, Negrito (Aeta), Subanon, and T'boli

LANGUAGES
National: Filipino (based on Tagalog)
Official: English
Bicolano, Cebuano, Hiligaynon, Ilocano, Kapampangan, Maguindanao, Tagalog, and Waray are the main regional languages or dialects.

RELIGIOUS GROUPS
Roman Catholics: 83 percent
Protestants: 9 percent
Muslims: 5 percent
Buddhists, Taoists, animists, and others make up the remaining 3 percent of the population.

HOLIDAYS
New Year's Day (January 1), Holy Week (March), Day of Valor (April 9), Labor Day (May 1), Independence Day (June 12), Manila Day (June 23), National Heroes' Day (August 31), All Saints' Day (November 1), Bonifacio Day (November 30), Christmas Day (December 25), and Rizal Day (December 30)

TIME LINE

IN THE PHILIPPINES	IN THE WORLD

250,000 B.C.
Dawn Man follows land bridges from Asia.

15,000 B.C.
Negrito become the first inhabitants.

3,000 B.C.
First Indonesians arrive by sea.

200 B.C.
Earliest Malayan sea immigrants

753 B.C.
Rome is founded.

116–17 B.C.
The Roman Empire reaches its greatest extent, under Emperor Trajan (98–17).

A.D. 600
Height of Mayan civilization

1000
The Chinese perfect gunpowder and begin to use it in warfare.

1521
Portuguese explorer Ferdinand Magellan reaches Cebu Island.

1530
Beginning of trans-Atlantic slave trade organized by the Portuguese in Africa.

1558–1603
Reign of Elizabeth I of England

1565
Miguel Lopez de Legazpi establishes a Spanish colony on Cebu Island.

1571
Manila is founded by Legazpi.

1762
British occupy Manila.

1620
Pilgrim Fathers sail the Mayflower to America.

1776
U.S. Declaration of Independence

1789–99
French Revolution

1861
U.S. Civil War begins.

1869
The Suez Canal is opened.

1872
Cavite Conspiracy; José Rizal leads Propaganda Movement.

1896
Rizal is executed; he becomes a national hero.

IN THE PHILIPPINES	IN THE WORLD
1898 Declaration of Independence; Spain cedes the Philippines to the U.S. for $20 million.	
1899 Aguinaldo proclaims the first Philippine Republic.	**1914** World War I begins.
1935 Start of 10-year Commonwealth	**1939** World War II begins.
1942 Manila falls to the Japanese.	
1944 U.S. forces regain Leyte; Philippine Commonwealth is reestablished.	**1945** The United States drops atomic bombs on Hiroshima and Nagasaki.
1946 U.S. grants the Philippines political independence.	**1949** North Atlantic Treaty Organization (NATO) is formed.
	1957 Russians launch Sputnik.
1965 Ferdinand Marcos is elected president; he is reelected four years later.	**1966–69** Chinese Cultural Revolution
1972 Marcos declares martial law.	
1985 Marcos calls for snap presidential elections; Corazon Aquino assumes the presidency.	**1986** Nuclear power disaster at Chernobyl in Ukraine
1991 Mount Pinatubo explodes.	**1991** Break-up of the Soviet Union
1992 Fidel Ramos is elected president; last U.S. naval vessel leaves Subic.	
1998 Joseph Estrada is elected president.	**1997** Hong Kong is returned to China.
2000 Gloria Arroyo is elected president.	**2001** World population surpasses 6 billion.

GLOSSARY

amor propio ("ah-MOR PRO-pio")
Self-esteem, similar to the concept of "face"

asuang ("AS-wahng")
A creature of the underworld

babaylan ("BA-BY-lun")
A faith healer or shaman

barangay ("ba-RUNG-gai")
Originally a pre-Spanish Filipino community, now still the basic unit of Philippine society and government

barong ("BA-rong")
Traditional wear for Filipino men

barrio ("BA-rio")
A village

cenaculo ("si-NAH-KU-loh")
The Philippine version of the passion play performed during Holy Week

compadrazgo ("COM-pud-DRAS-co")
Non-blood kinship ties usually established for baptisms, weddings, or any kind of sponsorship

delicadeza ("DE-lee-ka-DE-za")
Social propriety

galleon
A Spanish ship that sailed between Manila and Acapulco, laden with goods for Spain

hiya ("HEE-ya")
Shame

Indios
A derogatory term used by the Spanish colonial masters to refer to the indigenous Filipinos

karaoke
A leisure activity where people sing using a microphone, guided by music and lyrics; also the club in which people do this

kristo ("KRIS-to")
The ringmaster at a cockfight

Maria Clara
Dress worn by Filipinas, named after the main female character in José Rizal's *Noli Me Tangere*

mestizos ("mis-TEE-sos")
People of mixed ancestry

pakikisama ("pa-KI-ki-SUM-ma")
The art of maintaining smooth interpersonal relationships

pamanhikan ("PA-man-HEE-khan")
A formal proposal for a woman's hand in marriage

Pinoy ("PEE-noi")
The Filipinos' nickname for themselves

singkil ("SING-kil")
The traditional Philippine bamboo dance

FURTHER INFORMATION

BOOKS

Cootes, Jim, David P. Bank, and David Titmuss. *The Orchids of the Philippines*. Portland, Oregon: Timber Press, 2001.

De Villa, Jill Gale and Rebecca Gale De Villa. *Philippines Guide*. 2nd ed. New York: Open Road Publishing, 2000.

Dorai, Francis. *Insight Guide: Philippines*. Singapore: APA Publications, 2000.

Heaney, Lawrence R. and Jacinto C. Regalado, Jr. *Vanishing Treasures of the Philippine Rain Forest*. Chicago: University of Chicago Press, 1998.

Jealous, Virginia, et. al. *Lonely Planet Philippines*. 7th ed. California: Lonely Planet Publications, 2000.

Peplow, Evelyn and Alain Evrard. *The Philippines*. New York: Odyssey Publications, 1999.

Roces, Alfredo and Grace Roces. *Culture Shock! Philippines*. Portland, Oregon: Graphic Arts Center Pub. Co., 1992.

WEBSITES

Asian Development Bank (type "Philippines" in the search box). www.adb.org/default.asp

Central Intelligence Agency World Factbook (select Philippines from the country list). www.odci.gov/cia/publications/factbook/index.html

Library of Congress Country Study: Philippines. http://memory.loc.gov/frd/cs/phtoc.html

Lonely Planet World Guide: Destination Philippines. www.lonelyplanet.com/destinations/south_east_asia/philippines

National Geographic News "Still Green in Luzon." http://news.nationalgeographic.com/news/2000/12/1214_subicbay.html

National Statistical Coordination Board. www.nscb.gov.ph

Philippine culture and information. www.philinfo.ops.gov.ph

Philippine Department of Tourism. www.tourism.gov.ph

Philippine history. www.geocities.com/CollegePark/Pool/1644/precolonial.html

The World Bank Group (type "Philippines" in the search box). www.worldbank.org

MUSIC

Greetings from the Philippines. World Music Collection. PMF Records (Net), 1997.

Traditional Music from the Philippines. Fiesta Filipina. Arc (UK), 1999.

BIBLIOGRAPHY

Bjener, Tamiko. *Children of the World: Philippines*. Milwaukee: Gareth Stevens, 1987.

Fernando, Gilda. *We Live in the Philippines*. New York: Franklin Watts, 1986.

Fuentes, Vilma. *Pearl Makers: Six Stories about the Children in the Philippines*. New York: Friendship Press, 1989.

Haskins, James. *Corazon Aquino: Leader of the Philippines*. New Jersey: Enslow Publications, 1988.

Sonneborn, Liz. *The Philippines*. New York: Chelsea House, 1988.

INDEX